PRENTICE HALL
LITERATURE

Reader's COMPANION
English Learner's Version

The British Tradition

PEARSON

Prentice
Hall

Upper Saddle River, New Jersey
Needham, Massachusetts

Acknowledgments

Grateful acknowledgment is made to the following for copyrighted material:

Harlan Davidson Inc./Forum Press Inc.
Excerpt from "Book I" of *Utopia* by Thomas More, edited and translated by H. V. S. Ogden, pp. 21, 22 (Crofts Classics Series). Copyright © 1949 by Harlan Davidson, Inc.

Harcourt, Inc., and Faber and Faber Ltd.
"Journey of the Magi" from *Collected Poems 1909-1962* by T. S. Eliot, copyright 1936 by Harcourt, Inc., copyright © 1964, 1963 by T. S. Eliot.

Harcourt, Inc., and A. M. Heath & Co. Ltd.
From "Shooting an Elephant" from *Shooting an Elephant and Other Essays* by George Orwell, copyright 1950 by Sonia Brownell Orwell and renewed 1978 by Sonia Pitt-Rivers. Copyright © Mark Hamilton as the Literary Executor of the Estate of the Late Sonia Brownell Orwell and Martin Secker and Warburg Ltd.

George P. Landow
"The Victorian Web Overview" by George P. Landow from www.stg.brown. edu.

Dr. Peter F. Morgan c/o Alice Morgan
"Early Reviews of Wordsworth" from *Jeffrey's Criticism* by Francis Jeffrey, edited by Peter F. Morgan. Copyright © 1983 Peter F. Morgan.

The National Gallery, London
"The Gallery's Role and Objectives" by The National Gallery Department Office, from *The National Gallery's Roles and Objectives*.

New American Library, A division of Penguin Putnam, Inc.
From *Beowulf* by Burton Raffel, translator. Translation copyright © 1963 by Burton Raffel, Afterword © 1963 by New American Library.

Penguin Books Ltd.
From "The Prologue" to *The Canterbury Tales* by Geoffrey Chaucer, translated by Nevill Coghill (Penguin Classics 1951, Fourth revised edition 1977), copyright © 1951 by Nevill Coghill. Copyright © Nevill Coghill, 1958, 1960, 1975, 1977.

Simon & Schuster, Inc.
From "No Witchcraft for Sale," from *African Short Stories* by Doris Lessing. Copyright © 1951, 1953, 1954, 1957, 1958, 1962, 1963, 1964, 1965, 1972, 1981 by Doris Lessing.

University of Wisconsin Press
Excerpts from "The Defense of Poesy" from *Sir Philip Sidney: Selected Prose and Poetry*, edited by Robert Kimbrough. Copyright © 1969, 1983 by Robert Kimbrough.

Viking Penguin, Inc., a division of Penguin Putnam, Inc.
From "Araby", from *Dubliners* by James Joyce, copyright 1916 by B. W. Heubsch. Definitive text Copyright © 1967 by The Estate of James Joyce.

Note: Every effort has been made to locate the copyright owner of material reprinted in this book. Omissions brought to our attention will be corrected in subsequent editions.

Contents

Part 1: Selection Adaptations With Excerpts of Authentic Text 1

Unit 1: From Legend to History: The Old English and Medieval Periods (449–1485)

from **Beowulf** Translated by Burton Raffel . . . . **Epic** 4
from **The Canterbury Tales: The Prologue**
  Geoffrey Chaucer, Translated by Nevill Coghill . . . **Poem** 15
from **Morte d'Arthur** Sir Thomas Malory . . . . **Fiction** 26

Unit 2: Celebrating Humanity: The English Renaissance Period (1485–1625)

from **Utopia** Sir Thomas More . . . . **Fiction** 36
Speech Before Her Troops
  Queen Elizabeth I . . . . **Speech** 41
from **The Tragedy of Macbeth**
  William Shakespeare . . . . **Drama** 46

Unit 3: A Turbulent Time: The Seventeenth and Eighteenth Centuries (1625–1798)

Meditation 17 John Donne . . . . **Poem** 56
from **Paradise Lost** John Milton . . . . **Epic** 62
from **The Diary** Samuel Pepys . . . . **Nonfiction** 71
from **Gulliver's Travels** Jonathan Swift . . . . **Fiction** 80

Unit 4: Rebels and Dreamers: The Romantic Period (1798–1832)

Lines Composed a Few Miles Above Tintern Abbey
  William Wordsworth . . . . **Poem** 87
The Rime of the Ancient Mariner
  Samuel Taylor Coleridge . . . . **Poem** 95
Ode on a Grecian Urn John Keats . . . . **Poem** 104
from **A Vindication of the Rights of Woman**
  Mary Wollstonecraft . . . . **Nonfiction** 110

Unit 5: Progress and Decline: The Victorian Period (1833–1901)

The Lady of Shalott Alfred, Lord Tennyson . . . . . . **Poem** 116
My Last Duchess Robert Browning . . . . **Poem** 124
from **Hard Times** Charles Dickens . . . . **Fiction** 130
from **Jane Eyre** Charlotte Brontë . . . . **Fiction** 138

Unit 6: A Time of Rapid Change: The Modern and Postmodern Periods (1901–Present)

Journey of the Magi T. S. Eliot . . . . **Poem** 147
Shooting an Elephant George Orwell . . . . **Nonfiction** 153
No Witchcraft for Sale Doris Lessing . . . . **Short Story** 163
Araby James Joyce . . . . **Short Story** 174

Part 2: Reading Informational Materials **183**

Literary Map of Great Britain and Ireland . . . . Map 184
from **The Defense of Poesy** . . . . Position Statement 189
Letter on Light and Color . . . . Scientific Report 193
Early Reviews of Wordsworth . . . . Book Review 199
The Victorian Web . . . . Web Site 204
The National Gallery: Role and Objectives . . . . Mission Statement 208

Vocabulary Builder 214

Part 1

Selection Adaptations With Excerpts of Authentic Text

Part 1 will guide and support you as you interact with selections from *Prentice Hall Literature: Timeless Voices, Timeless Themes.* Part 1 provides summaries of literature selections with passages from the selection.

- Begin with the Preview page in the *English Learner's Companion.* Use the written and visual summaries to preview the selections before you read.

- Then study the Prepare to Read page. This page introduces skills that you will apply as you read selections in the *English Learner's Companion.*

- Now read the selection in the *English Learner's Companion.*

- Respond to all the questions along the sides as you read. They will guide you in understanding the selection and in applying the skills. Write in the *English Learner's Companion*—really! Circle things that interest you. Underline things that puzzle you. Number ideas or events to help you keep track of them. Look for the **Mark the Text** logo for help with active reading.

- Use the Review and Assess questions at the end of each selection to review what you have read and to check your understanding.

- Finally, do the Writing or the Speaking and Listening activity to extend your understanding and practice your skills.

Interacting With the Text

As you read, use the information and notes to guide you in interacting with the selection. The examples on these pages show you how to use the notes as a companion when you read. They will guide you in applying reading and literary skills and in thinking about the selections. When you read other texts, you can practice the thinking skills and strategies found here.

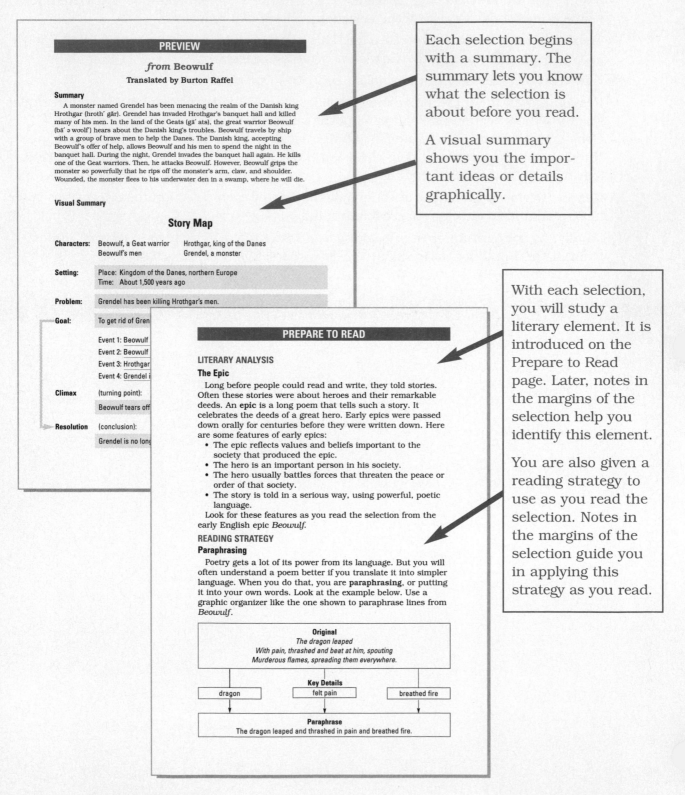

PREVIEW

from Beowulf
Translated by Burton Raffel

Summary

A monster named Grendel has been menacing the realm of the Danish king Hrothgar (hroth´ gär). Grendel has invaded Hrothgar's banquet hall and killed many of his men. In the land of the Geats (gā´ ats), the great warrior Beowulf (bā´ ə woolf´) hears about the Danish king's troubles. Beowulf travels by ship with a group of brave men to help the Danes. The Danish king, accepting Beowulf's offer of help, allows Beowulf and his men to spend the night in the banquet hall. During the night, Grendel invades the banquet hall again. He kills one of the Geat warriors. Then, he attacks Beowulf. However, Beowulf grips the monster so powerfully that he rips off the monster's arm, claw, and shoulder. Wounded, the monster flees to his underwater den in a swamp, where he will die.

Visual Summary

Story Map

| Characters: | Beowulf, a Geat warrior | Hrothgar, king of the Danes |
| | Beowulf's men | Grendel, a monster |

| Setting: | Place: Kingdom of the Danes, northern Europe |
| | Time: About 1,500 years ago |

| Problem: | Grendel has been killing Hrothgar's men. |

| Goal: | To get rid of Gren |

Event 1: Beowulf
Event 2: Beowulf
Event 3: Hrothgar
Event 4: Grendel i

| Climax | (turning point): |
| | Beowulf tears off |

| Resolution | (conclusion): |
| | Grendel is no lon |

Each selection begins with a summary. The summary lets you know what the selection is about before you read.

A visual summary shows you the important ideas or details graphically.

PREPARE TO READ

LITERARY ANALYSIS
The Epic

Long before people could read and write, they told stories. Often these stories were about heroes and their remarkable deeds. An **epic** is a long poem that tells such a story. It celebrates the deeds of a great hero. Early epics were passed down orally for centuries before they were written down. Here are some features of early epics:
- The epic reflects values and beliefs important to the society that produced the epic.
- The hero is an important person in his society.
- The hero usually battles forces that threaten the peace or order of that society.
- The story is told in a serious way, using powerful, poetic language.

Look for these features as you read the selection from the early English epic *Beowulf*.

READING STRATEGY
Paraphrasing

Poetry gets a lot of its power from its language. But you will often understand a poem better if you translate it into simpler language. When you do that, you are **paraphrasing**, or putting it into your own words. Look at the example below. Use a graphic organizer like the one shown to paraphrase lines from *Beowulf*.

Original
The dragon leaped
With pain, thrashed and beat at him, spouting
Murderous flames, spreading them everywhere.

Key Details

| dragon | felt pain | breathed fire |

Paraphrase
The dragon leaped and thrashed in pain and breathed fire.

With each selection, you will study a literary element. It is introduced on the Prepare to Read page. Later, notes in the margins of the selection help you identify this element.

You are also given a reading strategy to use as you read the selection. Notes in the margins of the selection guide you in applying this strategy as you read.

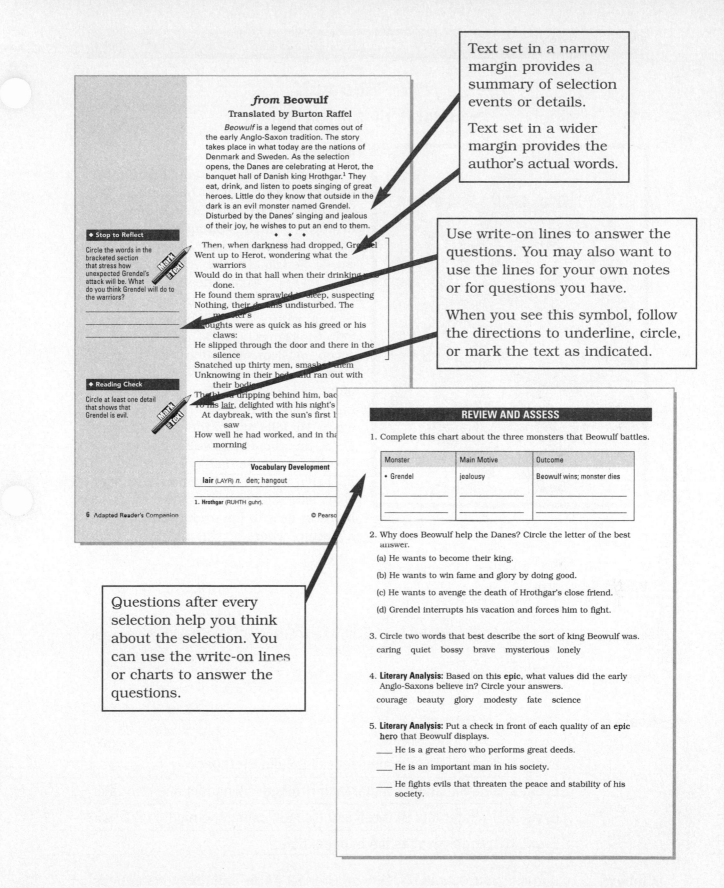

Text set in a narrow margin provides a summary of selection events or details.

Text set in a wider margin provides the author's actual words.

Use write-on lines to answer the questions. You may also want to use the lines for your own notes or for questions you have.

When you see this symbol, follow the directions to underline, circle, or mark the text as indicated.

Questions after every selection help you think about the selection. You can use the write-on lines or charts to answer the questions.

from **Beowulf**

Translated by Burton Raffel

Beowulf is a legend that comes out of the early Anglo-Saxon tradition. The story takes place in what today are the nations of Denmark and Sweden. As the selection opens, the Danes are celebrating at Herot, the banquet hall of Danish king Hrothgar.[1] They eat, drink, and listen to poets singing of great heroes. Little do they know that outside in the dark is an evil monster named Grendel. Disturbed by the Danes' singing and jealous of their joy, he wishes to put an end to them.

◆ ◆ ◆

Then, when darkness had dropped, Grendel
Went up to Herot, wondering what the warriors
Would do in that hall when their drinking was done.
He found them sprawled in sleep, suspecting
Nothing, their dreams undisturbed. The monster's
Thoughts were as quick as his greed or his claws:
He slipped through the door and there in the silence
Snatched up thirty men, smashed them
Unknowing in their beds and ran out with their bodies,
The blood dripping behind him, back to his lair, delighted with his night's
At daybreak, with the sun's first light,
How well he had worked, and in that morning

♦ Stop to Reflect

Circle the words in the bracketed section that stress how unexpected Grendel's attack will be. What do you think Grendel will do to the warriors?

_____

_____

_____

♦ Reading Check

Circle at least one detail that shows that Grendel is evil.

Vocabulary Development

lair (LAYR) *n.* den; hangout

1. **Hrothgar** (RUHTH guhr).

6 Adapted Reader's Companion

© Pearson

REVIEW AND ASSESS

1. Complete this chart about the three monsters that Beowulf battles.

Monster	Main Motive	Outcome
• Grendel	jealousy	Beowulf wins; monster dies

2. Why does Beowulf help the Danes? Circle the letter of the best answer.

(a) He wants to become their king.

(b) He wants to win fame and glory by doing good.

(c) He wants to avenge the death of Hrothgar's close friend.

(d) Grendel interrupts his vacation and forces him to fight.

3. Circle two words that best describe the sort of king Beowulf was.

caring   quiet   bossy   brave   mysterious   lonely

4. **Literary Analysis:** Based on this epic, what values did the early Anglo-Saxons believe in? Circle your answers.

courage   beauty   glory   modesty   fate   science

5. **Literary Analysis:** Put a check in front of each quality of an **epic hero** that Beowulf displays.

____ He is a great hero who performs great deeds.

____ He is an important man in his society.

____ He fights evils that threaten the peace and stability of his society.

from Beowulf

Translated by Burton Raffel

Summary

A monster named Grendel has been menacing the realm of the Danish king Hrothgar (hroth´ gär). Grendel has invaded Hrothgar's banquet hall and killed many of his men. In the land of the Geats (gā´ ats), the great warrior Beowulf (bā´ ə wŏolf´) hears about the Danish king's troubles. Beowulf travels by ship with a group of brave men to help the Danes. The Danish king, accepting Beowulf's offer of help, allows Beowulf and his men to spend the night in the banquet hall. During the night, Grendel invades the banquet hall again. He kills one of the Geat warriors. Then, he attacks Beowulf. However, Beowulf grips the monster so powerfully that he rips off the monster's arm, claw, and shoulder. Wounded, the monster flees to his underwater den in a swamp, where he will die.

Visual Summary

Setting:	Place: Kingdom of the Danes, northern Europe, about 1,500 years ago
Problem:	Grendel has been killing Hrothgar's men.
Goal:	To get rid of Grendel
	Event 1: Beowulf and his men set sail to help Hrothgar.
	Event 2: Beowulf and his men reach Hrothgar's kingdom and offer aid.
	Event 3: Hrothgar lets Beowulf and his men spend the night in the hall.
	Event 4: Grendel invades the banquet hall.
Climax:	(turning point): Beowulf tears off Grendel's arm, and the monster flees.
Resolution:	(conclusion): Grendel is no longer a threat to the kingdom.

LITERARY ANALYSIS

The Epic

Long before people could read and write, they told stories. Often these stories were about heroes and their remarkable deeds. An **epic** is a long poem that tells such a story. It celebrates the deeds of a great hero. Early epics were passed down orally for centuries before they were written down. Here are some features of early epics:

- The epic reflects values and beliefs important to the society that produced the epic.
- The hero is an important person in his society.
- The hero usually battles forces that threaten the peace or order of that society.
- The story is told in a serious way, using powerful, poetic language.

Look for these features as you read the selection from the early English epic *Beowulf.*

READING STRATEGY

Paraphrasing

Poetry gets a lot of its power from its language. But you will often understand a poem better if you translate it into simpler language. When you do that, you are **paraphrasing**, or putting it into your own words. Look at the example below. Use a graphic organizer like the one shown to paraphrase lines from *Beowulf.*

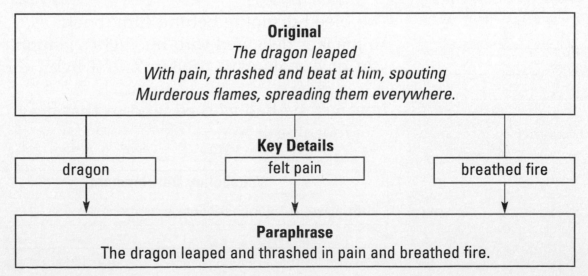

Original
The dragon leaped
With pain, thrashed and beat at him, spouting
Murderous flames, spreading them everywhere.

Key Details

| dragon | felt pain | breathed fire |

Paraphrase
The dragon leaped and thrashed in pain and breathed fire.

At the banquet at Herot, the
Danes are probably listening to
poems like *Beowulf*—epics
about heroes and their deeds.
What are some poems or songs
that celebrate heroes in your
native land? Write the name of
one on these lines. Be prepared
to tell classmates about it.

_____

_____

Homophones are
words with the same
sound but different
meanings and
spellings. Circle the
homophone for *there* that
appears a few lines down. Then,
write the meaning of each word.

there: _____

homophone: _____

meaning: _____

from Beowulf
Translated by Burton Raffel

Beowulf is a legend that comes out of
the early Anglo-Saxon tradition. The story
takes place in what today are the nations of
Denmark and Sweden. As the selection
opens, the Danes are celebrating at Herot, the
banquet hall of Danish king Hrothgar.[1] They
eat, drink, and listen to poets singing of great
heroes. Little do they know that outside in the
dark is an evil monster named Grendel.
Disturbed by the Danes' singing and jealous
of their joy, he wishes to put an end to them.

◆ ◆ ◆

Then, when darkness had dropped, Grendel
Went up to Herot, wondering what the
    warriors
Would do in that hall when their drinking was
    done.
He found them sprawled in sleep, suspecting
Nothing, their dreams undisturbed. The
    monster's
Thoughts were as quick as his greed or his
    claws:
He slipped through the door and <u>there</u> in the
    silence
Snatched up thirty men, smashed them
Unknowing in their beds and ran out with
    their bodies,
The blood dripping behind him, back
To his <u>lair</u>, delighted with his night's slaughter.
  At daybreak, with the sun's first light, they
    saw
How well he had worked, and in that gray
    morning

Vocabulary Development

lair (LAYR) *n.* den; hangout

---

1. **Hrothgar** (RUHTH guhr).

Broke their long feast with tears and laments
For the dead. Hrothgar, their lord, sat joyless
In Herot, a mighty prince mourning
The fate of his lost friends and companions,
Knowing by its tracks that some demon had
    torn
His followers apart. He wept, fearing
The beginning might not be the end. And that
    night
Grendel came again. . . .

◆   ◆   ◆

    For twelve long years, Grendel continues to attack the Danes. Stories of their sorrow reach across the sea to the land of the Geats,[2] where Beowulf, nephew of the Geat king, hears of the horror. Beowulf has already won fame and glory for his powerful fighting skills. Hoping to win more, he sails to the land of the Danes to help Hrothgar and his people. That night, Grendel attacks Herot again.

◆   ◆   ◆

Grendel snatched at the first Geat
He came to, ripped him apart, cut
His body to bits with powerful jaws,
Drank the blood from his veins and bolted
Him down, hands and feet; death
And Grendel's great teeth came together,
Snapping life shut. Then he stepped to another
Still body, clutched at Beowulf with his claws,
Grasped at a strong-hearted wakeful sleeper
—And was instantly seized himself, claws
Bent back as Beowulf leaned up on one arm.

Vocabulary Development

bolted (BOHL ted) *v.* swallowed

---

2. **Geats** (GAY atz) a people living in what today is the northern European nation of Sweden.

from Beowulf **7**

◆ Reading Strategy

Circle the letter of the choice below that best **paraphrases** the underlined lines.

(a) He cried because he has missed the start of the attack and could do little at the end.

(b) He cried because he was afraid there might be more attacks.

(c) He cried because he feared a different monster would come.

(d) He cried because his rule of Denmark was beginning to end.

◆ English Language Development

From earliest times, English speakers liked to take several descriptive words and shorten them into a **compound adjective**. Here, for example, "sleeper *with a strong heart*" has become "*strong-hearted* sleeper." On the lines below, turn each wordy phrase into a compound adjective before a noun.

blade with a steel edge:

_____

dragon who breathes fire:

_____

Who is the "shepherd of evil" and "guardian of crime"? Write the character's name: _____
The words *evil* and *crime* stress that he does bad things. What do *shepherd* and *guardian* stress? Circle the letter of your answer.

(a) He does not mean to do bad.

(b) He protects others when he can.

(c) He is in charge of doing bad things.

(d) He does bad things in both the country and the city.

◆ **Reading Check**

What has happened here? Circle the letter of the best answer below.

(a) Beowulf failed to kill Grendel, who crawls off to fight another day.

(b) Having received a fatal wound, Grendel crawls off to die.

(c) Beowulf killed Grendel on the spot and now goes to Grendel's den.

(d) Beowulf and Grendel fought to a draw and will now make peace.

◆ **Vocabulary and Pronunciation**

The word *sword* rhymes with *poured.* Say the word aloud, and circle the silent letter.

That shepherd of evil, guardian of crime,
Knew at once that nowhere on earth
Had he met a man whose hands were harder;
His mind was flooded with fear—but nothing
Could take his talons and himself from that
      tight
Hard grip. . . .
The monster's hatred rose higher,
But his power had gone. He twisted in pain,
And the bleeding sinews deep in his shoulder
Snapped, muscle and bone split
And broke. The battle was over. Beowulf
Had been granted new glory: Grendel
      escaped,
But wounded as he was could flee to his den,
His miserable hole at the bottom of the
      marsh
Only to die. . . .

◆ ◆ ◆

The Danes are delighted by Grendel's death and honor Beowulf that night in celebrations. But another monster still threatens them—Grendel's mother. Outraged by her son's death, she attacks Herot that very night. She kills Hrothgar's friend and then returns to her lair at the bottom of the lake. Beowulf bravely follows.

◆ ◆ ◆

Then he saw
The mighty water witch and swung his sword,
His ring-marked blade, straight at her
      head; . . .

Vocabulary Development

talons (TA luhnz) *n.* claws
sinews (SIN yooz) *n.* tendons; cords that connect muscles to bones and other body parts

---

But her guest
Discovered that no sword could slice her evil
Skin, that Hrunting[3] could not hurt her, was useless
Now when he needed it. They wrestled, she ripped
And tore and clawed at him, bit holes in his helmet,
And that too failed him; for the first time in years
Of being worn to war it would earn no glory;
It was the last time anyone would wear it. But Beowulf
Longed only for fame, leaped back
Into battle. He tossed his sword aside,
Angry; the steel-edged blade lay where
He'd dropped it. If weapons were useless he'd use
His hands, the strength in his fingers. So fame
Comes to men who mean to win it
And care about nothing else! . . .
 Then he saw, hanging on the wall, a heavy
Sword, hammered by giants, strong
And blessed with their magic, the best of all weapons
But so massive that no ordinary man could lift
Its carved and decorated length. He drew it
From its scabbard, broke the chain on its hilt,
And then, savage, now, angry
And desperate, lifted it high over his head

3. **Hrunting** (RUHNT ing) the name of Beowulf's sword. Valuable swords were often given names.

© Pearson Education, Inc.

from Beowulf **9**

And struck with all the strength he had left,
Caught her in the neck and cut it through,
Broke bones and all. Her body fell
To the floor, lifeless, the sword was wet
With her blood, and Beowulf <u>rejoiced</u> at the
    sight.

❖   ❖   ❖

After being honored by Hrothgar,
Beowulf and the other Geats return home.
There Beowulf eventually becomes king. He
rules with success for fifty years. Then a
Geat man steals a drinking cup from a
treasure in a tower guarded by a fire-
breathing dragon. When the angry dragon
attacks his kingdom, Beowulf, despite old
age, goes to battle the creature.

❖   ❖   ❖

Then Beowulf rose, still brave, still strong,
And with his shield at his side, and a mail
    shirt[4] on his breast,
<u>Strode</u> calmly, confidently, toward the tower,
    under
The rocky cliffs; no coward could have walked
    there! . . .
The <u>beast</u> rose, angry,
Knowing a man had come—and then nothing
But war could have followed. Its breath came
    first,
A steaming cloud pouring from the stone,
Then the earth itself shook. Beowulf
Swung his shield into place. . . .

Vocabulary Development

rejoiced (re JOYST) *v.* took joy in; was happy
strode (STROHD) *v.* walked

---

4. **mail shirt** a shirt made out of metal links that give protection in battle.

The Geats'
Great prince stood firm, unmoving, prepared
Behind his high shield, waiting in his
    shining
Armor. The monster came quickly toward
    him,
Pouring out fire and smoke, hurrying
To its fate. Flames beat at the iron
Shield, and for a time it held, protected
Beowulf as he'd planned; then it began to melt,
And for the first time in his life that famous
    prince
Fought with fate against him, with glory
Denied him. He knew it, but he raised his
    sword
And struck at the dragon's scaly hide.
The ancient blade broke, bit into
The monster's skin, drew blood, but
    cracked
And failed him before it went deep enough,
    helped him
Less than he needed. <u>The dragon leaped</u>
<u>With pain, thrashed and beat at him,</u>
    <u>spouting</u>
<u>Murderous flames, spreading them</u>
    <u>everywhere</u>.

◆ ◆ ◆

All of Beowulf's subjects have fled in
terror except Wiglaf, who fights at Beowulf's
side. But though Beowulf manages to kill the
dragon, he receives a fatal wound himself.
Gasping, he reminds Wiglaf to claim the
dragon's treasure for the Geats. He then
gives his final instructions.

◆ ◆ ◆

◆ **Literary Analysis**

Circle the detail that shows
the early Anglo-Saxon
belief in fate guiding
human affairs. Based on
this passage, what other
values does this **epic**
reflect?

_____

_____

_____

◆ **Reading Strategy**

Paraphrase the underlined
sentence. Write it on these lines
in your own words.

_____

_____

_____

_____

Vocabulary Development

thrashed (THRASHT) *v.* moved wildly

The word *tomb*, which refers to a burial place, rhymes with *room*. The *b* is silent. A *b* is almost always silent when it comes after *m* at the end of a word. If the *mb* comes earlier in a word, the *b* is sometimes pronounced. Say these words aloud.

bomb	combine	dumb
bomber	crumb	numb
comb	crumble	tombstone

◆ Culture Note

Like the epic itself, the tower named for Beowulf is a form of lasting fame to honor him after he dies. What are some things today that we often name in honor of people who have died?

_____

_____

_____

◆ Literary Analysis

Based on this closing portion of the **epic**, what do the early Anglo-Saxons seem to admire in their leaders?

_____

_____

_____

"Wiglaf, lead my people,
Help them; my time is gone. Have
The brave Geats build me a <u>tomb</u>,
When the funeral flames have burned me, and
    build it
Here, at the water's edge, high
On this <u>spit</u> of land, so sailors can see
This tower, and remember my name, and
    call it
Beowulf's tower. . . ."
    Then the Geats built the tower, as Beowulf
Had asked, strong and tall, so sailors
Could find it from far and wide; working
For ten long days they made his monument,
Sealed his ashes in walls as straight
And high as wise and willing hands
Could raise them. And the riches he and Wiglaf
Had won from the dragon, rings, necklaces,
Ancient, hammered armor—all
The treasures they'd taken were left there, too,
Silver and jewels buried in the sandy
Ground, back in the earth, again
And forever hidden and useless to men.
And then twelve of the bravest Geats
Rode their horses around the tower,
Telling their sorrow, telling stories
Of their dead king and his greatness, his glory,
Praising him for heroic deeds, for a life
As noble as his name, . . .
Crying that no better king had ever
Lived, no prince so mild, no man
So open to his people, so deserving of praise.

Vocabulary Development

spit (SPIT) *n.* a narrow point of land

---

1. Complete this chart about the three monsters that Beowulf battles.

Monster	Main Motive	Outcome
• Grendel	jealousy	Beowulf wins; monster dies
_____	_____	_____
_____	_____	_____

2. Why does Beowulf help the Danes? Circle the letter of the best answer.

   (a) He wants to become their king.

   (b) He wants to win fame and glory by doing good.

   (c) He wants to avenge the death of Hrothgar's close friend.

   (d) Grendel interrupts his vacation and forces him to fight.

3. Circle two words that best describe the sort of king Beowulf was.

   caring   quiet   bossy   brave   mysterious   lonely

4. **Literary Analysis:** Based on this **epic**, what values did the early Anglo-Saxons believe in? Circle your answers.

   courage   beauty   glory   modesty   fate   science

5. **Literary Analysis:** Put a check in front of each quality of an **epic hero** that Beowulf displays.

   ____ He is a great hero who performs great deeds.

   ____ He is an important man in his society.

   ____ He fights evils that threaten the peace and stability of his society.

from Beowulf **13**

6. **Reading Strategy:** Circle the letter of the choice below that best **paraphrases** these three lines from Beowulf:

That shepherd of evil, guardian of crime,

Knew at once that nowhere on earth

Had he met a man whose hands were harder. . .

(a) Beowulf knew he had never shaken anyone's hand more firmly.

(b) Grendel knew he had never fought harder.

(c) Grendel knew he had never met a man who was stronger.

(d) The dragon knew he had never faced and fought anyone older.

Listening and Speaking

Dramatic Reading

Give a dramatic reading of a passage from Beowulf, such as the battle with Grendel's mother or the death of Beowulf.

- Practice your reading with a partner.

- Try to speak clearly at an appropriate pace or speed.

- Try to capture the right tone for the lines you are reading. For example, if the details in a line are exciting, try to sound excited.

- When you feel you are ready, perform the passage for classmates.

from The Canterbury Tales: The Prologue

Geoffrey Chaucer

Translated by Nevill Coghill

Summary

On April 11, 1387, the author joins a diverse group of pilgrims at an inn just outside of London. Together they will journey to the shrine of St. Thomas à Becket at Canterbury Cathedral in southeastern England. Their purpose is to honor this saint, who was murdered in the cathedral in 1170. The characters in the group represent a cross section of medieval society. Among them are a knight and his son, who is a squire or knight's helper; a yeoman, who is a servant to the squire; a nun, accompanied by another nun and three priests; a well-dressed monk; a jolly friar, a member of a religious order; a merchant; a clergyman who is an impoverished student; and a number of others. The host of the inn devises a plan for each pilgrim to tell two stories on the way to Canterbury and two stories on the way back.

Visual Summary

Characters:	Traits and Appearance
1. Knight	distinguished; fought in crusades; wise; modest; coarse clothes
2. Squire	knight's son; about 20; lover; strong and agile; sings; plays flute
3. Yeoman	squire's servant; green clothes; bow and arrow; woodsman
4. Nun	high rank; dainty; speaks French; good manners; tender heart
5. Monk	manly man; good rider; likes to hunt; wears fine clothes
6. Friar	merry; good talker; takes gifts to forgive sins; good singer
7. Merchant	divided beard; pompous; hides fact he is in debt
8. Oxford Cleric	thin; has no money; loves to read, learn, and teach

LITERARY ANALYSIS

Characterization

Authors use **characterization** to create and develop a character's personality.

- In **direct characterization,** the author makes direct statements about a character's personality and attitudes. For example, in the Prologue, Chaucer directly states that the Parson was "a holy-minded man."
- In **indirection characterization,** personality and attitudes are revealed through a character's actions and speech. For instance, we also learn that the Parson knows and preaches religious teachings. From these details, we can conclude that the Parson is a religious, or "holy-minded," man.

As you read the Prologue to *The Canterbury Tales*, look for examples of both direct and indirect characterization.

READING STRATEGY

Analyzing Difficult Sentences

Poetry can contain long sentences that are hard to follow. When you **analyze difficult sentences,** you figure out the main points that the sentences are trying to make. To figure out the main points, use the questions *Who, What, When, Where, Why,* and *How?*

Who?
There was a Knight, a most distinguished man,

When?
Who from the day on which he first began

What?
To ride abroad had followed chivalry . . . .

As you read Chaucer's Prologue, analyze long, difficult sentences by using these questions to focus on their main points.

from The Prologue to The Canterbury Tales

Geoffrey Chaucer

People in the Middle Ages often made holy journeys, or pilgrimages, to the city of Canterbury to honor Archbishop Thomas á Becket, killed in 1170. One <u>April</u> in the 1300's, a group of pilgrims, or travelers making this pilgrimage, met at the Tabard Inn just outside London. Chaucer describes each pilgrim, starting with a Knight.

♦ ♦ ♦

There was a <u>Knight</u>, a most distinguished man,
Who from the day on which he first began
To ride abroad had followed chivalry,[1]
Truth, honor, generousness and courtesy.
He had done nobly in his sovereign's[2] war
And ridden into battle, no man more . . .

♦ ♦ ♦

The Knight has fought in the Crusades, the Christian holy wars to gain control of Jerusalem. He makes his pilgrimage to give thanks for surviving. With him is his son, a knight-in-training, or Squire, of about twenty. The Squire likes to joust, or fight in tournaments, but he also likes music, poetry, and showy clothes.

♦ ♦ ♦

He was embroidered like a meadow bright
And full of freshest flowers, red and white.
Singing he was, or fluting all the day;
He was as fresh as is the month of May.
Short was his gown, the sleeves were long and wide;
He knew the way to sit a horse and ride.

---

1. chivalry (SHIV uhl ree) *n.* the code of behavior for knights, which stressed truth, honor, generosity, and courtesy.
2. sovereign's (SOV ruhnz) ruler's; king's.

Remember that in English, the twelve months of the year each begin with a capital letter. Write them in order on the lines below.

_____ _____

_____ _____

_____ _____

April_____ _____

_____ _____

_____ _____

In the Middle English spoken in Chaucer's day, the *k* before the *n* in *knight* was pronounced. Today, it is silent. Circle the other letters that are silent in the word *knight*. What other word sounds the same as *knight* but is spelled differently and has a different meaning?

_____

_____

After the Normans, who spoke a type of French, conquered England in 1066, their ruling class introduced many French words into English. Many of these words have to do with the king's court, the law, and upper-class life. *Chivalry,* the knights' code of honor, comes from French, as does *courtesy,* which originally meant "polite behavior expected in a royal or noble court." In the bracketed passage, circle the part of *courtesy* that shows this original meaning.

◆ Culture Note

The French spoken in Paris was considered the most proper.

(1) What can you assume about the French the Nun speaks?

_____

_____

_____

(2) Why do you think the Nun tries to speak French at all?

_____

_____

_____

He could make songs and poems and recite,
Knew how to joust and dance, to draw and
   write.

◆ ◆ ◆

   The Knight also travels with a Yeoman (YOH man) dressed like a forest hunter. The Yeoman serves as the Knight's attendant. Next Chaucer describes a Nun who is Prioress (PRĪ uhr uhs), or assistant head, of the nunnery where she lives.

◆ ◆ ◆

And she was known as Madam Eglantyne.
And well she sang a service,[3] with a fine
Intoning through her nose, as was most
   seemly,
And she spoke daintily in French, extremely,
After the school of Stratford-atte-Bowe;[4]
French in the Paris style she did not know.
At meat[5] her manners were well taught withal;[6]
No morsel from her lips did she let fall,
Nor dipped her fingers in the sauce too deep;
But she could carry a morsel up and keep
The smallest drop from falling on her breast.
For courtliness she had a special zest,
And she would wipe her upper lip so clean
That not a trace of grease was to be seen.

◆ ◆ ◆

   The Nun's group includes another Nun and several Priests. There are also other members of the clergy going to Canterbury.

◆ ◆ ◆

Vocabulary Development

intoning (in TOHN ing) *n.* chanting; humming
seemly (SEEM lee) *adv.* proper; fitting
morsel (MOHR suhl) *n.* small bite or piece
courtliness (KOHRT lee nuhs) *n.* elegant manners

---

3. **service** daily prayer.
4. **Stratford-atte-Bowe** a nunnery near London.
5. **At meat** at meals.
6. **withal** (with AWL) *adv.* in addition; nevertheless; besides.

A Monk there was, one of the finest sort
Who rode the country; hunting was his sport.
A manly man, to be an Abbot[7] able;
Many a dainty horse he had in stable.
His bridle, when he rode, a man might hear
Jingling in a whistling wind as clear,
Aye, and as loud as does the chapel bell
Where my lord Monk was Prior of the cell.[8]
The Rule of good St. Benet or St. Maur[9]
As old and strict he tended to ignore;
He let go by the things of yesterday
And took the modern world's more spacious way.

◆ ◆ ◆

Next there is a Friar, or begging Monk, who likes the company of innkeepers and barmaids far more than that of the poor. And there is a Merchant who seems so successful that no one knows he is in debt. In contrast is the Oxford Cleric, a student of religion at Oxford University. He cares only about his study and his faith.

◆ ◆ ◆

Whatever money from his friends he took
He spent on learning or another book
And prayed for them most <u>earnestly</u>, returning
Thanks to them thus for paying for his learning.
His only care was study, and indeed
He never spoke a word more than was need,
Formal at that, respectful in the extreme,
Short to the point, and <u>lofty</u> in his theme.

Vocabulary Development

earnestly (ER nuhst lee) *adv.* in a sincere way
lofty (LAWF tee) *adj.* elevated; high minded; idealistic

---

7. **Abbot** (AB uht) *n.* a monk in charge of a monastery, or community of monks.
8. **Prior** (PRĪ uhr) **of the cell** head of a smaller monastery that is part of a larger one.
9. **St. Benet** (buh NAY) **and St. Maur** (MAWR) the French names for St. Benedict, who established the rules for monks, and St. Maurice, one of his followers.

© Pearson Education, Inc.

Poetry sometimes uses unusual word order. For example:

Chaucer's order: A Monk there was.

Usual order: There was a Monk.

Rewrite the following sentences using more usual word order.

Chaucer's order: Many a dainty horse he had in stable.

Usual order:

_____

_____

_____

Chaucer's order: His bridle, when he rode, a man might hear jingling in a whistling wind.

Usual order:

_____

_____

_____

Chaucer's order: The Rule of good St. Benet or St. Maur as old and strict he tended to ignore.

Usual order:

_____

_____

_____

Learn and *teach* are sometimes confused. To *teach* is to provide information; to *learn* is to find it out. Complete each sentence below by circling the correct verb in parentheses. Notice that the past tense of *teach* is *taught.*

(1) I (learned, taught) to read some Middle English, the language in which Chaucer wrote.

(2) A professor (learned, taught) me several Middle English words.

(3) The professor will (learn, teach) me more words tomorrow.

In English, two vowels often combine to form a single sound. For example, in the word *measure,* the *ea* sounds like the short /e/ in *bed.* Sometimes, however, two vowels in a row do not combine; instead, they each have a separate sound. In *diet,* the *i* has a long /i/ sound, like the *i* in *ride.* But the *e* has its own separate sound, the unstressed vowel sound of the *e* in *taken.* Circle two more words in the bracketed passage in which two vowels in a row have their own separate sounds. Also say the words aloud.

The thought of moral virtue filled his speech
And he would gladly <u>learn</u>, and gladly <u>teach</u>.

◆ ◆ ◆

There is also a Sergeant at the Law, a lawyer for the king's courts; a Franklin, or wealthy landowner; a Skipper, or ship's captain; a Cook; and several tradesmen—a Weaver, a Carpenter, a Carpet Maker, and others. Then there is a Doctor skilled in the medical practices of the day.

◆ ◆ ◆

In his own <u>diet</u> he observed some <u>measure</u>;
There were no superfluities[10] for pleasure,
Only digestives, nutritives[11] and such.
He did not read the Bible very much.
In blood-red garments, slashed with bluish-gray
And lined with taffeta,[12] he rode his way;
Yet he was rather <u>close</u> as to expenses
And kept the gold he won in <u>pestilences</u>.
<u>Gold stimulates the heart, or so we're told</u>.
<u>He therefore had a special love of gold</u>.

◆ ◆ ◆

Also traveling to Canterbury is a woman from the English city of Bath, and a Parson, or village priest. The woman, known as the Wife of Bath, has been married and widowed five times. She now spends her days making pilgrimages all over Europe and the Middle East.

◆ ◆ ◆

Vocabulary Development

close (KLOHS) *adj.* Stingy
pestilences (PES tuh luhn siz) *n.* Contagious diseases; plagues

---

10. **superfluities** (soo puhr FLOO uh teez) *n.* things that are not necessities.
11. **digestives** (duh JES tivs), **nutritives** (NOO truh tivs) foods eaten because they are healthy.
12. **taffeta** (TAF uh tuh) *n.* a fine silk fabric.

Easily on an <u>ambling</u> horse she sat
Well wimpled up,[13] and on her head a hat
As broad as is a buckler[14] or a shield;
She had a flowing mantle[15] that concealed
Large hips, her heels spurred sharply under that.
In company she liked to laugh and chat
And knew the remedies for love's
    <u>mischances</u>,
An art in which she knew the oldest dances.
A holy-minded man of good <u>renown</u>
There was, and poor, the Parson to a town,
Yet he was rich in holy thought and work.
He also was a learned man, a clerk,
Who truly knew Christ's gospel[16] and would
    preach it
<u>Devoutly</u> to <u>parishioners</u>, and teach it.

◆   ◆   ◆

Traveling with the Parson is his honest,
hard-working brother, a farmer or Plowman. A
bit less honest is the Miller, a jolly fellow with
a red beard and a wart at the end of his nose.

◆   ◆   ◆

His nostrils were as black as they were wide.
He had a sword and buckler at his side,
His mighty mouth was like a furnace door.

Vocabulary Development

ambling (AM bling) *adj.* moving at a slow, easy speed
mischances (mis CHAN siz) *n.* unlucky accidents;
    misfortunes
renown (ree NOWN) *n.* fame
devoutly (duh VOWT lee) *adv.* in a religious way
parishioners (puh RISH uhn uhrz) *n.* churchgoers in the
    priest's district

◆ **Literary Analysis**

Circle one example each of **direct** and **indirect** **characterization** in these bracketed lines. Label them *direct* or *indirect*. What do they reveal about the personality or attitudes of the Wife of Bath or the Parson?

(1) The Wife of Bath is

_____

_____

(2) The Parson is

_____

_____

◆ **Reading Check**

Because of her great experience with love, what does the Wife of Bath know?

_____

_____

_____

---

13. **wimpled** (WIM puhld) **up** wearing a scarf covering the head, neck, and chin, as was customary for married women.
14. **buckler** (BUCK luhr) *n.* small round shield.
15. **mantle** (MAN tuhl) *n.* cloak.
16. **gospel** (GOS puhl) a part of the Bible that tells of Christ's life and teachings.

© Pearson Education, Inc.   *from* The Prologue to The Canterbury Tales **21**

Thumb, the word for the thickest, shortest finger, rhymes with *gum;* the *b* is silent. A *b* is often silent after an *m,* but not if it starts a new syllable. In *combine,* for example, the *b* starts a new syllable and is pronounced. Say *thumb* and *combine* aloud. Then practice saying all the words below. Circle any silent *b.*

bomb	dumb	limber
bumble	lamb	tomb
climber	limb	tombstone

◆ Reading Check

What musical instrument does the Miller play as the pilgrims leave the town?

_____

A wrangler and buffoon,[17] he had a store
Of tavern stories, filthy in the main.[18]
His was a master-hand at stealing grain.
He felt it with his <u>thumb</u> and thus he knew
Its quality and took three times his due—
A thumb of gold, by God, to <u>gauge</u> an oat!
He wore a hood of blue and a white coat.
He liked to play his bagpipes up and down
And that was how he brought us out of town.

◆ ◆ ◆

    The Manciple, or caterer, works at one of the London law schools. Though not a learned man, he manages to cheat all the clever law students. The Reeve, or estate manager, is skilled at managing his master's wealth. He has also managed to stash away quite a bit for himself. The Summoner, who summons people to appear in Church court, is a heavy drinker with a bad complexion. His companion is a Pardoner, an official who sells papal pardons to those summoned to the court. The Pardoner also claims to own several holy relics, or items associated with Jesus, Mary, and the saints.

◆ ◆ ◆

For in his trunk he had a pillowcase
Which he asserted was Our Lady's veil.[19]
He said he had a gobbet[20] of the sail
Saint Peter had the time when he made bold
To walk the waves, till Jesu Christ took hold.
He had a cross of metal set with stones
And, in a glass, a rubble of pigs' bones.

Vocabulary Development

gauge (GAYJ) *v.* measure; weigh

---

17. **wrangler** (RANG luhr) **and buffoon** (buh FOON) someone who often argues or clowns around.
18. **in the main** mainly; for the most part.
19. **Our Lady's veil** (VAYL) a veil worn by Mary, mother of Jesus.
20. **gobbet** (GOB it) *n.* piece.

And with these relics, any time he found
Some poor up-country parson to astound,
On one short day, in money down, he drew
More than the parson in a month or two,
And by his flatteries and <u>prevarication</u>
Made <u>monkeys</u> of the priest and congregation.

◆ ◆ ◆

Having now described everyone,
Chaucer tells of the merry meal at the Tabard
Inn before the group leaves for Canterbury.
The Innkeeper joins the fun and makes an
interesting offer.

◆ ◆ ◆

"My lords," he said, "now listen for your good,
And please don't treat my notion with <u>disdain</u>.
This is the point. I'll make it short and plain.
Each one of you shall help to make things slip[21]
By telling two stories on the outward trip
To Canterbury, that's what I intend,
And, on the homeward way to journey's end
Another two, tales from the days of old;
And then the man whose story is best told,
That is to say who gives the fullest measure
Of good morality and general pleasure,
He shall be given a supper, paid by all,
Here in this tavern, in this very hall,
When we come back again from Canterbury.
And in the hope to keep you bright and merry
I'll go along with you myself and ride
All at my own expense and serve as guide.
I'll be the judge, and those who won't obey
Shall pay for what we spend upon the way."

◆ ◆ ◆

Everyone is happy to agree to the
Innkeeper's offer. The stories the pilgrims tell
become the individual stories of the rest of
The Canterbury Tales.

Vocabulary Development

prevarication (pree var uh KAY shuhn) *n.* avoiding the truth
disdain (dis DAYN) *n.* scorn; contempt

---

21. **make things slip** make the time go faster.

1. On the chart below, list two characters that Chaucer seems to praise and two that he seems to criticize.

Praises	Criticizes

2. What do the Nun Prioress, the Monk, and the Pardoner all have in common? Circle the letter of the correct answer.

   (a) They are all deeply religious officials of the Church.

   (b) Despite their Church ties, they all have worldly concerns.

   (c) They are all rude and uneducated.

   (d) They all cheat and steal from others.

3. What activity that people do today seems most like the pilgrimage Chaucer describes? Circle the letter of the best answer.

   (a) praying   (c) taking a bus tour on vacation

   (b) watching TV   (d) visiting family members

4. **Reading Strategy:** Use questions such as *What, Where, When, Why,* and *How* to help you **analyze difficult sentences** in the Host's speech near the end of the selection. Then, describe the Host's plan for the journey.

   _____

   _____

   _____

   _____

5. **Literary Analysis:** Based on both **direct and indirect characterization**, match each character with his or her description. Write the letter of the description on the line before the character's name. Use each description only once.

____ Knight		a. very scholarly
____ Squire		b. poor, holy, and sincere
____ Nun Prioress		c. stingy and careful about his health
____ Monk		d. talkative and learned in the ways of love
____ Oxford Cleric		e. worldly sportsman
____ Doctor		f. religious faker
____ Miller		g. loyal and brave soldier
____ Wife of Bath		h. pretentious; tries to seem elegant
____ Parson		i. young, artistic, and romantic
____ Pardoner		j. dishonest and coarse or vulgar

Listening and Speaking

A Conversation

Working with two partners, create a conversation that three of Chaucer's characters might have had about their trip.

1. Choose the characters you will play.

2. Reread the sections of the Prologue describing your characters.

3. Jot down details about your character's personality and attitudes.

Character	
Personality	
Reason for making the trip	
Attitude toward the trip	

4. Begin your conversation. As you play your part, express ideas and attitudes that you think are appropriate to your character.

from Morte d'Arthur

Sir Thomas Malory

Summary

King Arthur returns to England to fight with Sir Mordred, his nephew, who has seized control of the kingdom. Sir Gawain, recently killed, appears to Arthur in a dream and warns him that he will be slain if he fights with Mordred. Arthur tries to arrange a truce. However, a knight draws a sword to kill a snake, and the armies begin fighting. Arthur slays Mordred but is badly wounded.

Weakened, Arthur tells Sir Bedivere to throw Arthur's sword, Excalibur, into the water. After failing twice, Bedivere throws the sword. It is caught by a hand that takes it away under the waves. Then, Bedivere helps Arthur into a boat in which there are many beautiful women. Arthur tells Bedivere that he is going to the island of Avilion to be healed.

Next morning, Bedivere finds a chapel and a newly dug grave. A hermit tells Bedivere that, at midnight, a number of beautiful women brought him a body to bury. Bedivere assumes that this was Arthur's body.

Visual Summary

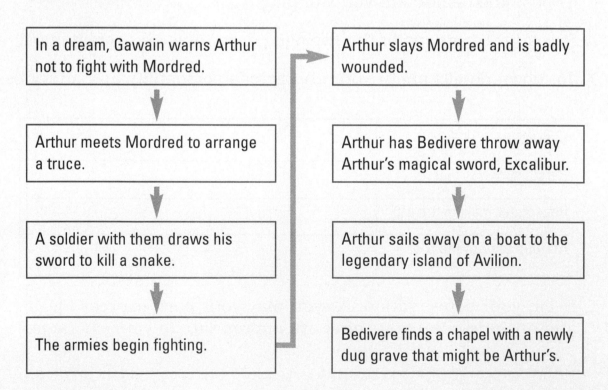

In a dream, Gawain warns Arthur not to fight with Mordred.

↓

Arthur meets Mordred to arrange a truce.

↓

A soldier with them draws his sword to kill a snake.

↓

The armies begin fighting.

→

Arthur slays Mordred and is badly wounded.

↓

Arthur has Bedivere throw away Arthur's magical sword, Excalibur.

↓

Arthur sails away on a boat to the legendary island of Avilion.

↓

Bedivere finds a chapel with a newly dug grave that might be Arthur's.

LITERARY ANALYSIS
Medieval Romance

A **medieval** (mee DEE vuhl) **romance** is an adventure story from the Middle Ages. It often contains some or all of these elements:
- unusual or exotic settings
- magical or supernatural events
- high-born figures, such as kings and queens
- brave knights
- beautiful ladies, often in need of help
- battles, quests, contests, and tests
- themes of love, loyalty, faith, and courage

The most famous medieval romances are probably those about King Arthur and his court. As you read this selection from *Morte d'Arthur*, look for elements of medieval romance.

READING STRATEGY
Summarizing

One way to understand and remember important information is to summarize what you read. **Summarizing** means giving just the main ideas and key details briefly in your own words. Below is passage from *Morte d'Arthur* with main ideas and details highlighted and a summary underneath. As you read the selection, summarize other passages to keep track of key ideas and details.

Passage

. . . and there King Arthur smote Sir Mordred under the shield, with a thrust of his spear, throughout the body more than a fathom. And when Sir Mordred felt that he had his death's wound, he thrust himself with the might that he had up to the burr of King Arthur's spear, and right so he smote his father King Arthur with his sword holden in both his hands, upon the side of the head, that the sword pierced the helmet and the casing of the brain.

Summary

Arthur gives Mordred a deadly wound, and Mordred responds by wounding Arthur fatally.

---

from Morte d' Arthur **27**

from Morte d' Arthur
Sir Thomas Malory

♦ **Culture Note**

During the Middle Ages, knights swore loyalty to their lord or king. Breaking that oath of loyalty was a great sin. Mordred's close family relationship to Arthur make his sin even worse. What is his relationship to Gawain, who dies because of his actions?

_____

_____

_____

♦ **English Language Development**

Morte d'Arthur uses many old words not usually used today. What pronoun is used today instead of *ye?* Use the surrounding words to figure out the meaning of *ye.*

_____

_____

_____

Then, to help you read this paragraph, cross out all the *ye's* and write the modern pronoun instead.

King Arthur creates an ideal kingdom called Camelot where talented knights sit at a Round Table and all feel equal. But jealousy and other human weakness eventually destroy Camelot. Arthur is forced to fight his friend Sir Lancelot in France. While he is away, his illegitimate son Mordred tries to steal the English throne. When Arthur races home to fight Mordred, Arthur's nephew Sir Gawain is killed almost immediately. Gawain returns to Arthur in a dream, surrounded by lovely ladies Gawain has helped in life. He warns Arthur not to fight Mordred the next day. If he does, both sides will take huge losses, and Arthur will die. So Arthur arranges a one-month treaty. The two sides each bring fourteen men to the place where the treaty will be signed.

♦ ♦ ♦

And when King Arthur should depart, he warned all his <u>host</u> that, and[1] they see any sword drawn, "Look <u>ye</u> come on fiercely and <u>slay</u> that traitor Sir Mordred, for I in no wise[2] trust him." In like wise Sir Mordred warned his host that "And ye see any manner of sword drawn, look that ye come on fiercely, and so slay all that ever before you standeth, for in no wise I will not trust for this treaty." And in the same wise said Sir Mordred unto his host, "For I know well my father will be <u>avenged</u> upon me."

Vocabulary Development

host (HOHST) *n.* army; troops
slay (SLAY) *v.* kill
avenged (uh VENJD) *v.* gotten revenge

---

1. **and** if.
2. **wise** way.

And so they met as their pointment[3] was and wcrc agreed and <u>accorded</u> thoroughly. And wine was fetched and they drank together. Right so came an <u>adder</u> out of a little heath-bush, and it stung a knight in the foot. And so when the knight felt him so stung, he looked down and saw the adder. And anon[4] he drew his sword to slay the adder, and thought none other harm. And when the host on both parties saw that sword drawn, then they blew beams,[5] trumpets, horns, and shouted grimly. And so both hosts dressed them[6] together. And King Arthur took his horse and said, "Alas, this unhappy day!" and so rode to his party, and Sir Mordred in like wise.

◆ ◆ ◆

The battle that breaks out is a horrible one. A hundred thousand soldiers are killed. Arthur is horrified to see so many of his noble knights fall.

◆ ◆ ◆

Then King Arthur looked about and was ware[7] where stood Sir Mordred leaning upon his sword among a <u>great heap of dead</u> men.
"Now give me my spear," said King Arthur unto Sir Lucan, "for yonder I have <u>espied</u> the traitor that all this woe hath wrought."[8]

◆ ◆ ◆

◆ Reading Strategy

Circle key ideas and details in the bracketed passage. Then, **summarize** how the fighting begins.

_____

_____

_____

◆ Vocabulary and Pronunciation

The letter combination *ea* has three main sounds, shown on this chart. Say the three examples aloud.

Sound	Example	Rhymes with
1. long /*a*/	great	ate
2. long /*e*/	heap	peep
3. short /*e*/	dead	bed

Say each word below. Then, on the line, write whether it uses long /*a*/, long /*e*/, or short /*e*/.

- already _____
- jealous _____
- break _____
- spear _____
- death _____
- steak _____
- dream _____
- treaty _____

Vocabulary Development

accorded (uh KAWR did) *v.* brought into harmony or agreement

adder (AD uhr) *n.* poisonous snake

espied (es PĪD) *v.* spotted; seen

---

3. **pointment** arrangement.
4. **anon** soon after; immediately.
5. **beams** a type of trumpet.
6. **dressed them** prepared to come.
7. **ware** aware.
8. **hath wrought** (RAWT): has made.

© Pearson Education, Inc.

from Morte d' Arthur **29**

Read the underlined sentence aloud. How do you think Arthur said it? Circle the letter of the best choice below. Then circle the punctuation in the underlined sentence that points to the answer.

(a) in a loud, angry voice

(b) in a tired, weary voice

(c) in a frightened, trembling voice

(d) in a dangerously quiet voice

◆ **English Language Development**

A famous English spelling rule says:

Use i *before* e *except after* c

Or when sounded like A *as in* neighbor *and* weigh.

Of course, there are exceptions, but *shield* follows the rule. So do all the incomplete words below. Complete each by adding *ie* or *ei* on the line. Also say the words aloud.

bel___ve   f___rce   rec___ve

c___ling   gr___ve   shr___k

dec___ve   p___rced   v___l

◆ **Vocabulary and Pronunciation**

The word *wound* has two different pronunciations. Rhymed with *ground,* it means "twisted or turned." Rhymed with *tuned,* it means "an injury" or "to injure."

(1) What is the word's meaning here?

_____

(2) How should the word be pronounced here?

_____

Sir Lucan, one of Arthur's knights, advises him not to fight. He points out that Arthur has already won the day and reminds the king of his dream. But Arthur insists on fighting Mordred.

◆　◆　◆

Then the King got his spear in both his hands and ran toward Sir Mordred, crying and saying, "<u>Traitor, now is thy deathday come!</u>"

And when Sir Mordred saw King Arthur he ran until him with his sword drawn in his hand, and there King Arthur <u>smote</u> Sir Mordred under the <u>shield</u>, with a thrust of his spear, throughout the body more than a fathom.[9] And when Sir Mordred felt that he had his death's <u>wound</u>, he thrust himself with the might that he had up to the burr[10] of King Arthur's spear, and right so he smote his father King Arthur with his sword holden in both his hands, upon the side of the head, that the sword pierced the helmet and the casing of the brain. And therewith Sir Mordred dashed down stark dead to the earth.

And noble King Arthur fell in a swough[11] to the earth, and there he <u>swooned</u> oftentimes, and Sir Lucan and Sir Bedivere ofttimes heaved him up. And so, weakly betwixt[12] them, they led him to a little chapel not far from the seaside.

◆　◆　◆

Vocabulary Development

smote (SMOHT) *v.* struck down or killed; past tense of *smite*

swooned (SWOOND) *v.* fainted

---

9. **fathom** (FATH uhm) *n.* six feet.
10. **burr** hand guard.
11. **swough** (SWŌ) *n.* faint or swoon.
12. **betwixt** (buh TWIXT) *prep.* between.

Sir Lucan and his brother Sir Bedivere decide to bring the wounded Arthur to the safety of a town. They try to lift him up again. But Lucan, who was wounded in battle, collapses and dies. Bedivere weeps at the death of his brother and the likely death of his king.

◆ ◆ ◆

"Now leave this mourning and weeping gentle knight," said the King, "for all this will not avail me.[13] For wit thou[14] well, and might I live myself, the death of Sir Lucan would grieve me evermore. But my time passeth on fast," said the King. "Therefore," said King Arthur unto Sir Bedivere, "take thou here <u>Excalibur</u> my good sword and go with it to yonder water's side; and when <u>thou comest there I charge thee</u> throw my sword in that water and come again and tell me what thou sawest there."

"My lord," said Sir Bedivere, "your <u>commandment</u> shall be done, and I shall lightly[15] bring you word again."

◆ ◆ ◆

Sir Bedivere takes the sword to the lake. But he cannot bring himself to throw it in. It simply seems too valuable. There are even jewels in the hilt, or handle. So Bedivere hides the sword under a tree and returns to Arthur.

◆ ◆ ◆

"What saw thou there?" said the King.

"Sir," he said, "I saw nothing but waves and winds."

"That is untruly said of thee," said the King. "And therefore go thou lightly again and do my commandment; as thou art to me loved and dear, spare not, but throw it in."

◆ ◆ ◆

Vocabulary Development

commandment (kuh MAND muhnt) *n.* order; command

---

13. **avail** (uh VAYL) **me** help me; do me any good.
14. **wit thou** know you.
15. **lightly** quickly.

from Morte d' Arthur **31**

◆ **Culture Note**

In the early Middle Ages, it was the custom of warriors to give a name to their sword. Why do you think they did this?

_____

_____

_____

◆ **English Language Development**

Thou and *thee* are two more old forms of *you,* and *passeth* is an old verb form that would be *passes* today. The selection uses several old verb forms ending in *eth* or *est.* Circle two more in this paragraph. Near each, write the verb form that would be used today.

Sir Bedivere goes again to the lake. He still cannot throw the sword in. Again he returns to Arthur and pretends he has thrown it in. Again Arthur knows he is lying. Arthur begs Bedivere to obey him.

◆ ◆ ◆

<u>Then Sir Bedivere departed and went to the sword and lightly took it up, and so he went to the water's side; and there he bound the girdle[16] about the hilts, and threw the sword as far into the water as he might. And there came an arm and an hand above the water and took it and clutched it, and shook it thrice[17] and brandished; and then vanished away the hand with the sword into the water.</u> So Sir Bedivere came again to the King and told him what he saw.

"Alas," said the King, "help me hence,[18] for I dread me[19] I have <u>tarried</u> overlong."

Then Sir Bedivere took the King upon his back and so went with him to that water's side. And when they were at the water's side, even fast[20] by the <u>bank</u> floated a little <u>barge</u> with many <u>fair</u> ladies in it; and among them all was a queen; and all they had black hoods, and all they wept and shrieked when they saw King Arthur.

Vocabulary Development

brandished (BRAN disht) *v.* waved in a threatening way

tarried (TAR eed) *v.* waited; lingered

bank (BANK) *n.* the land alongside a lake or river

barge (BAHRJ) *n.* a flat-bottomed boat

fair (FAYR) *adj.* pretty; nice looking

---

16. **girdle** (GER duhl) *n.* the sash or belt used to strap the sword around the hips of the person wearing it.
17. **thrice** (THRĪS) *adv.* three times.
18. **hence** from here.
19. **dread** (DRED) **me** fear.
20. **fast** close.

"Now put me into that barge," said the King; and so he did softly. And there received him three ladies with great mourning, and so they set them down. And in one of their laps King Arthur laid his head.

◆ ◆ ◆

Sir Bedivere weeps as Arthur explains that he must leave him and go to the legendary island of Avilion. He asks Bedivere to pray for him. The next morning, Bedivere meets a hermit who was once the Archbishop of Canterbury. The hermit explains that some women brought him a dead body. They asked him to bury it. So the hermit buried it in the little chapel.

◆ ◆ ◆

Now more of the death of King Arthur could I never find, but that these ladies brought him to his grave, and such one was <u>interred</u> there which the hermit bare witness that was once Bishop of Canterbury. But yet the hermit knew not in certain that he was verily[21] the body of King Arthur; for this tale Sir Bedivere, a knight of the Table Round, made it to be written.

Yet some men say in many parts of England that King Arthur is not dead, but carried by the will of our Lord Jesu into another place; and men say that he shall come again, and he shall win the Holy Cross. Yet I will not say that it shall be so, but rather I would say: here in this world he changed his life. And many men say that there is written upon the tomb this:

HIC IACET ARTHURUS, REX QUONDAM, REXQUE FUTURUS[22]

◆ Reading Check

According to the ending, what has happened or will happen to Arthur? Answer by completing the sentence below.

Either he

_____

_____

_____

or he

_____

_____

_____

Vocabulary Development

interred (in TURD) *n.* buried

---

21. **verily** (VER uh lee) *adv.* truly.
22. **HIC . . . FUTURS** Here lies Arthur, who was once king and will be king again.

© Pearson Education, Inc.

1. What does Arthur's dream suggest about events in the rest of the selection? Circle the letter of the best answer.

   (a) The events are all a dream from which Arthur wakes in the end.

   (b) Arthur's death is in the hands of fate, predicted in advance.

   (c) Mordred is really the rightful king of England.

   (d) Sir Gawain is responsible for all the fighting.

2. Circle all the qualities that King Arthur seems to display.

   shyness   leadership   honor   courage   stinginess

3. What causes the fighting when Arthur and Mordred are trying to establish peace?

   _____

   _____

4. **Literary Analysis:** On the chart, list an example of each element of a medieval romance.

Element	Example
unusual or exotic settings	
magical or supernatural events	
high-born figures	
brave knights	
beautiful ladies	
battles, quests, contests, or tests	
themes of love, loyalty, faith, courage	

5. **Reading Strategy:** Summarize what happens to Arthur's sword.

   _____

   _____

Writing

An Interior Monologue

An **interior monologue** shows a character's thoughts and feelings. Write a brief interior monologue showing Sir Bedivere's thoughts and feelings when he tries to throw the sword into the lake.

- List the actual events in sequence.

First, Sir Bedivere

_____

_____ .

Next, Sir Bedivere

_____

_____ .

Finally, Sir Bedivere

_____

_____ .

- Jot down what Sir Bedivere's thoughts might be during each event.

First, he thinks

_____

_____ .

Next, he thinks

_____

_____ .

Finally, he thinks

_____

_____ .

- On separate paper, write your interior monologue.

from Utopia

Sir Thomas More

Visual Summary

Summary

Subjects choose a king for their own sake, not for the king's. A king should therefore take better care of his subjects than he does of himself. By keeping his subjects poor, a king will only make them more discontent. He should live on the income that he naturally receives and not seize property from his subjects in an unjust manner. Also, he should deal with crime by preventing it, rather than by punishing criminals after they have violated the law.

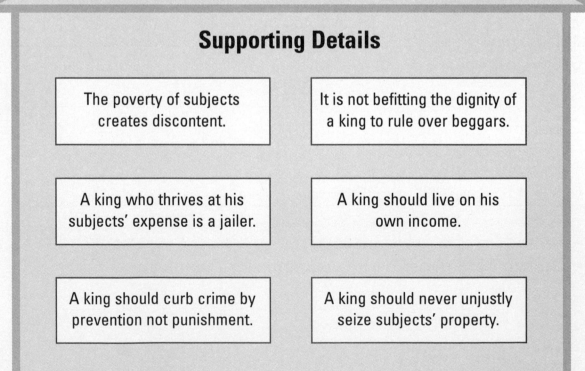

Main Idea

Because people choose a king for their own sake,
a king should take better care of his subjects than of himself.

Supporting Details

The poverty of subjects creates discontent.	It is not befitting the dignity of a king to rule over beggars.
A king who thrives at his subjects' expense is a jailer.	A king should live on his own income.
A king should curb crime by prevention not punishment.	A king should never unjustly seize subjects' property.

LITERARY ANALYSIS

Theme: The Monarch as Hero

The word *Renaissance* means rebirth. During the Renaissance period in England (1485-1625), there was a series of strong monarchs, or rulers. Under these rulers, both kings and queens, England became a powerful country. Culture and the arts also flourished.

The literature of the English Renaissance contains many examples of the **monarch as hero**. In these portraits in words, the ruler is a courageous, noble person, larger than life. Writers probably created these heroic portraits for several reasons:

- Rulers shown as heroes would inspire confidence and loyalty in citizens.
- Praising rulers in power could help a writer establish strong connections at court.

As you read this selection, look for passages that reflect the **theme** of the monarch as hero.

READING STRATEGY

Summarizing

To understand a difficult work, **summarize** the main points of your reading. When you summarize, you use your own words to state the main ideas and key details of a passage. An effective summary is always much shorter than the original.

As you read this selection, track the main ideas with a chart.

Sentence in More's Original Text
He ought to shake off either his sloth or his pride, for the people's hatred and scorn arise from these faults in him.

↓

Summary/Main Idea
A good king should not be lazy or proud, or the people will hate him.

In a **summary,** you state the main idea of a passage in your own words. Summarize More's main idea in the bracketed passage.

_____

_____

_____

◆ English Language Development

More believes that the answers to the questions in the bracketed passage are obvious. He uses the questions for persuasive effect. Rewrite one of the three questions so that it is in the form of a statement, rather than a question.

_____

_____

_____

◆ Literary Analysis

Underline two words or phrases that More uses to describe people who are the *opposite* of a **monarch as hero.**

◆ Reading Check

Circle two words identifying vices or defects that cause the people to hate or scorn a ruler.

from Utopia
Sir Thomas More

A good king should be like a shepherd. He should care for his people's happiness more than for his own.

◆ ◆ ◆

Certainly it is wrong to think that the poverty of the people is a safeguard of public peace. Who quarrel more than beggars do? Who long for a change more earnestly than the dissatisfied? Or who rushes in to create disorders [with] such desperate boldness as the man who has nothing to lose and everything to gain?

◆ ◆ ◆

If a king is hated by his subjects, it is better for him to resign. Dignified kings rule over happy and prosperous people, not over beggars.

◆ ◆ ◆

When a ruler enjoys wealth and pleasure while all about him are grieving and groaning, he acts as a jailor rather than as a king. He is a poor physician who cannot cure a disease except by throwing his patient into another. A king who can only rule his people by taking from them the pleasures of life shows that he does not know how to govern free men. He ought to shake off either his <u>sloth</u> or his pride, for the people's hatred and scorn arise from these faults in him. Let him live on his own income without wronging others, and limit his expenses to his <u>revenue</u>.

◆ ◆ ◆

A good king should try to prevent crime. He should not try foolishly to revive outdated laws. He should never take other people's property in cases where a judge would decide that such a seizure was evil.

Vocabulary Development

sloth (SLOHTH) *n.* laziness
revenue (REV uh nyoo) *n.* income

1. On the lines below, write two reasons More gives for thinking that poverty is a threat to a nation.

   Reason 1: _____

   Reason 2: _____

2. According to More, when does a king become like a jailor?

   _____

   _____

3. How does More appeal to the self-interest of rulers to strengthen his argument?

   _____

   _____

   _____

4. **Literary Analysis:** In portraits of the **monarch as hero**, the ruler is a perfect person. According to More, why should a ruler be careful to exercise restraint and self-control?

   _____

   _____

   _____

5. **Reading Strategy:** In a **summary,** you use your own words to state the main ideas and key details of a passage. What general rules or principles for good leadership does More present in the passage from *Utopia?* Begin your summary of the passage by completing the sentence shown on the lines below.

   A good ruler should _____

   _____.

Listening and Speaking

A Debate

In a **debate,** two individual speakers or groups of speakers argue the opposite sides of a question or issue. A debate usually has a formal structure, with rules about the order of the presentations and time limits for the speakers. Most formal debates are held in front of an audience. Sometimes the listeners vote at the end of the debate, choosing the side they think has been more persuasive.

Form two groups and prepare for a debate on this question:

Do More's ideas in *Utopia* apply to today's leaders?

1. Which side of the debate will you choose? Check one.

      PRO (answering YES to the question)   ❑

      CON (answering NO to the question)   ❑

2. In a debate, your goal is to persuade your listeners to adopt your point of view. Successful persuasion depends on a number of techniques. In your debate, use the following persuasive devices:

Persuasive Devices	Examples from More
• strong arguments, supported by reasons, facts, or examples	
• emotional appeals to the feelings of your listeners	
• language charged with strong overtones or associations	
• vivid images	

3. Prepare a three-minute presentation supporting the side you have chosen.
4. When both groups, Pro and Con, have prepared presentations, hold your debate before the class.
5. Ask your classmates to vote on which group was more persuasive.

Speech Before Her Troops
Queen Elizabeth I

Summary

Queen Elizabeth is speaking to her armed forces, who have assembled to do battle with the Spanish fleet, known as the Spanish Armada. She tells her audience that she has been advised not to appear before them, for fear that she might be attacked. However, she trusts her loyal subjects. She wants to be among them at this critical moment and, if necessary, to lay down her life. She may "have . . . the body of a weak . . . woman," but she has the brave "heart of a . . . king of England, . . ." Also, she will reward those who fight well. She tells her listeners to obey her lieutenant general, who will lead the English forces. Then, she predicts that they will soon win a great victory over the Spanish.

Visual Summary

Two Strands of Queen Elizabeth's Argument

Arguments for Dramatic Effect

- Some say that I should be afraid to mingle with my own soldiers.

- Because I am not a tyrant, I will never be afraid of my own loyal subjects.

- I have come here to say that I have the "heart of a . . . king of England" and will, if necessary, die in the battle.

Practical Message

- I will reward you for your brave deeds.

- Obey my lieutenant general, who will act for me in the battle.

- Through your brave deeds and obedience, we will soon win a great victory.

LITERARY ANALYSIS

Theme: The Monarch as Hero

During the English Renaissance (1485-1625), a series of strong kings and queens ruled England. Under these rulers, England became a powerful country. Culture and the arts flourished.

English literature of this period contains many portrayals of a king or queen, **or monarch, as hero.** The monarch is described as courageous and noble, sometimes even larger than life. Writers probably created these heroic descriptions for several reasons:

- Monarchs shown as heroes would inspire confidence and loyalty in citizens.
- Praising monarchs could help a writer establish strong connections at court.

As you read this selection, look for passages that reflect the **theme** of the monarch as hero.

READING STRATEGY

Summarizing

Sometimes you must read a work written in an unfamiliar style. Sometimes it is difficult to understand new subject matter. To understand an unfamiliar or difficult work, **summarize** the main points of your reading. When you summarize, you use your own words to state the main ideas and key details of a passage. A good summary is always much shorter than the original.

As you read this selection, find and summarize the main ideas with a chart like the one shown.

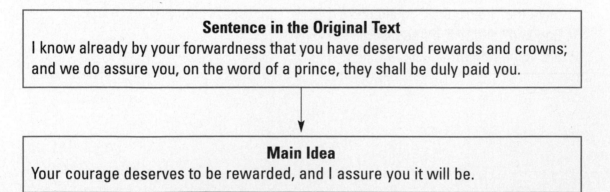

Sentence in the Original Text
I know already by your forwardness that you have deserved rewards and crowns; and we do assure you, on the word of a prince, they shall be duly paid you.

↓

Main Idea
Your courage deserves to be rewarded, and I assure you it will be.

Speech Before Her Troops
Elizabeth I

My loving people, we have been persuaded by some, that are careful of our safety, to take heed how we commit ourselves to armed multitudes, for fear of <u>treachery</u>; but I assure you, I do not desire to live to distrust my faithful and loving people. Let tyrants fear; I have always so behaved myself that, under God, I have placed my chiefest strength and safeguard in the loyal hearts and good will of my subjects.

◆ ◆ ◆

Therefore, says Elizabeth, she has come before the troops. She has made a firm decision to live or die with them. She will lay down her honor and her life for God and for the kingdom.

◆ ◆ ◆

[I know I have but the body of a weak and feeble woman; but I have the heart of a king, and of a king of England, too.

◆ ◆ ◆

It is disgraceful that any foreign ruler should dare to invade England. Elizabeth says she will fight rather than suffer dishonor. She herself will lead her troops in battle, and she will reward her soldiers for bravery.

◆ ◆ ◆

I know already, by your forwardness, that you have deserved rewards and crowns; and we do assure you, on the word of a prince, that they shall be duly paid you.

◆ ◆ ◆

The lieutenant who represents Elizabeth is noble and worthy. She tells the troops she is sure that their obedience, teamwork, and courage will help them defeat the enemy. They will win a famous victory.

Vocabulary Development

treachery (TRECH uhr ee) *n.*   betrayal of trust or faith

◆ Vocabulary and Pronunciation

Elizabeth I uses the pronoun *we* rather than *I* to refer to herself. This usage is sometimes called the "royal *we.*" You will also find it used by courtroom judges and newspaper editors. What effect does this choice of words have?

_____

_____

◆ Reading Strategy

Summarize, or restate briefly in your own words, the first paragraph of Elizabeth's speech.

_____

_____

_____

_____

_____

◆ Literary Analysis

How does the comparison in the bracketed paragraph show Elizabeth as a **heroic monarch?**

_____

_____

_____

◆ Stop to Reflect

What effect do you think this speech had on Queen Elizabeth's audience?

_____

_____

_____

1. What does Elizabeth say her advisors have warned her not to do?

_____

_____

2. Why has Elizabeth not listened to her advisors?

_____

_____

3. What does Elizabeth promise to do rather than let her country be dishonored?

_____

_____

4. **Reading Strategy:** When you **summarize** a passage, you use your own words to state the main idea. Summarize the contrast that Elizabeth draws between herself and tyrants.

_____

_____

5. **Literary Analysis:** In portrayals of the **monarch as hero,** the ruler is courageous and larger-than-life. Elizabeth says, "I know I have but the body of a weak and feeble woman; but I have the heart of a king, and of a king of England, too." Explain how this statement relates to the idea of a heroic monarch.

_____

_____

Writing

A Letter to the Editor

Queen Elizabeth I has definite ideas about the characteristics of a good leader. For example, she believes that an effective leader should

- not distrust or fear the people.
- be prepared to make sacrifices for the common good.
- be courageous and fight enemies when necessary.
- reward the people for their support and effort.

A **letter to the editor** expresses your opinion on a current topic or issue. After stating your position, you support it with persuasive devices, such as facts, examples, or reasons.

Write a letter to the editor in which you apply Elizabeth's standards for good leadership to one of today's leaders, such as a president, a prime minister, or a governor. As you work on this assignment, follow these steps:

1. Choose a modern leader. _____

2. Use the library or the Internet to find new stories about the modern leader. Take notes on his or her leadership skills as shown in the news stories.

Elizabeth I	_____
does not distrust or fear the people	
is prepared to make sacrifices for the common good	
is courageous and fights enemies when necessary	
rewards the people for their support and effort	

3. On separate paper, write a draft of your letter. Start by stating Elizabeth I's ideas of leadership. Then show how her standards apply to the modern leader you have chosen.

4. Reread the draft of your letter. Add or move details if necessary to make your arguments stronger.

5. Share your letter with your classmates by posting it on the class bulletin board.

from The Tragedy of Macbeth

William Shakespeare

Summary

In Act I, we learn that the Scottish nobleman Macbeth has fought well in a battle. Returning from the battlefield, he and his fellow nobleman Banquo (baŋk´ wō) meet three witches. The witches predict that Macbeth will not only be rewarded by King Duncan of Scotland but will become king himself. However, the witches also greet Banquo as a father of kings. Macbeth considers killing Duncan, who will visit Macbeth's castle. In Act II, Scene i, Macbeth learns that Banquo will not support him in anything dishonorable.

After killing Duncan, Macbeth kills Banquo. However, Banquo's son, Fleance (flē´ äns), escapes. Macbeth also kills the family of Macduff, who has fled to England. In England, Macduff joins with Malcolm, Duncan's son. Prince Malcolm is assembling an army to take back Scotland from Macbeth. Meanwhile, Macbeth learns from the three witches that he should fear Macduff but need not fear any man born of woman. Macbeth also learns that he need not worry until the forest itself marches against him. However, in Act V, Macbeth's forces are defeated by Malcolm's army and Macbeth is killed by Macduff.

Visual Summary

Act I: Exposition	Act II: Rising Action	Act III: Climax	Act IV: Falling Action	Act V: Resolution
Macbeth does well in battle; he and Banquo meet three witches, who predict that Macbeth will be king and Banquo will be father of kings; Macbeth and Lady Macbeth plot to kill King Duncan, who is visiting their castle.	When Banquo reveals he will not do anything dishonorable, Macbeth hides his plan from him; Macbeth and Lady Macbeth kill Duncan.	Macbeth plots to kill Banquo and his son, Fleance, but Fleance escapes; Macbeth sees Banquo's ghost at a feast; Macbeth vows that he will continue in evil and wants to see the witches again.	The witches tell Macbeth to (1) fear no man (2) fear Macduff (3) have no fears until the forest marches against you; Macbeth kills Macduff's family; Macduff, in England, joins with Malcolm, Duncan's son.	Malcolm's army marches against Macbeth's army and defeats it; Macduff kills Macbeth in hand-to-hand combat; Malcolm becomes the rightful king of Scotland.

LITERARY ANALYSIS

Shakespearean Tragedy

Shakespearean tragedy usually contains these elements:

- A central character of high rank and outstanding abilities, but with a **tragic flaw**, or weakness
- A chain of related events that lead this character to disaster, at least partly through his or her flaw
- Lively action that creates a vivid spectacle

As they watch the downfall of the central character, members of the play's audience feel a mixture of pity, fear, and awe. These feelings lift them out of their everyday lives. These emotions are stirred when the tragic hero confronts his or her limits in a noble way.

As you read this play, look for elements of Shakespearean tragedy.

READING STRATEGY

Reading Verse for Meaning

To **read verse for meaning**, read sentences rather than lines. For instance, you must follow this sentence past the end of the line to find out what the speaker fears:

Hear not my steps, which way they walk, for fear
Thy very stones prate of my whereabout . . . (II, i, 17-18)

As you read, use a chart to distinguish between lines and sentences.

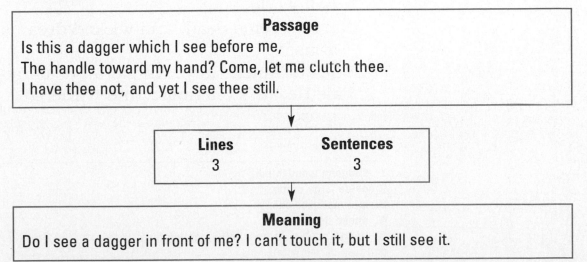

Passage
Is this a dagger which I see before me,
The handle toward my hand? Come, let me clutch thee.
I have thee not, and yet I see thee still.

Lines	Sentences
3	3

Meaning
Do I see a dagger in front of me? I can't touch it, but I still see it.

from **Macbeth**
William Shakespeare

Macbeth, a Scottish nobleman and general, meets three mysterious witches. They predict that he will rule Scotland one day as king. Macbeth's wife urges him to assassinate King Duncan while the king is visiting them. At night, Macbeth prepares for the murder. First he dismisses his servant.

◆　◆　◆

MACBETH. Go bid thy mistress, when my
  drink is ready,
She strike upon the bell. Get thee to bed.
                    [*Exit* servant.]
Is this a dagger which I see before me,
The handle toward my hand? Come, let me
  clutch thee.
5 I have thee not, and yet I see thee still.

◆　◆　◆

    Macbeth wonders if the dagger is real
or imaginary.

◆　◆　◆

              I see thee still,
And on thy blade and dudgeon[1] gouts[2] of
  blood,
Which was not so before. There's no such
  thing.
It is the bloody business which informs[3]
10 Thus to mine eyes. Now o'er the one
  half-world
Nature seems dead, and wicked dreams
  abuse[4]
The curtained sleep; witchcraft celebrates
Pale Hecate's offerings;[5] and withered
  murder,

---

1. **dudgeon** wooden hilt.
2. **gouts** large drops.
3. **informs** takes shape.
4. **abuse** deceive.
5. **Hecate's** (HEK uh teez) **offerings** offerings to Hecate, the Greek goddess of witchcraft.

◆ **Vocabulary and Pronunciation**

Shakespeare often uses the archaic or old-fashioned forms *thy, thee,* and *thou.* If *thy* means "your," what do *thee* and *thou* mean?

thee: _____

thou: _____

◆ **Reading Check**

Underline the words that show how the dagger's appearance has changed.

Alarumed[6] by his <u>sentinel</u>, the wolf,
15 Whose howl's his watch, thus with his
    <u>stealthy</u> pace,
With Tarquin's[7] ravishing strides, towards
    his design
Moves like a ghost. Thou sure and firm-set
    earth,
Hear not my steps, which way they walk,
    for fear
Thy very stones prate[8] of my whereabout,
20 And take the present horror from the time,
Which now suits with it.[9] Whiles I threat,
    he lives:
Words to the heat of deeds too cold breath
    gives.

                [*A bell rings.*]
I go, and it is done: the bell invites me.
Hear it not, Duncan, for it is a knell
25 That summons thee to heaven, or to hell.
                [*Exit.*]
              ◆   ◆   ◆

Macbeth murders King Duncan. After
Macbeth is crowned king, he and Lady
Macbeth cling to power through bloodshed
and tyranny. Macbeth has one of his fellow
generals murdered. Fearing the nobleman
Macduff, Macbeth orders the murders of
Macduff's wife and children. Macduff and
Malcolm, the rightful heir to the throne, raise
a rebel army. The witches tell Macbeth that
he does not need to fear until Birnam Wood
moves toward the castle at Dunsinane. Also,

Vocabulary Development

sentinel (SENT uh nuhl) *n.* guard; watchman
stealthy (STEL thee) *adj.* sly

---

6. **Alarumed** (uh LAR uhmd): urged on to battle.
7. **Tarquin's** of Tarquin, an ancient Roman tyrant.
8. **prate** chatter; talk idly.
9. **and . . . it** remove the horrible silence which suits this moment.

© Pearson Education, Inc.

from Macbeth **49**

◆ **Reading Strategy**

When you read **verse for meaning,** how many sentences do you find in the bracketed passage?

_____

_____

◆ **English Language Development**

In English, writers often use vivid figures of speech, or expressions that are not meant to be taken literally. Shakespeare uses many figures of speech. Here he compares murder to a person. What does this person look like, and how does he move?

_____

_____

_____

◆ **Stop to Reflect**

What does Macbeth mean by his statement about words and deeds in line 22?

_____

_____

◆ **Read Fluently**

Read lines 23-25 aloud.

1. Why does the bell sound?

_____

_____

2. In Macbeth's imagination, what has the bell now become?

_____

3. Underline the words that give the answer.

they say, Macbeth will not be defeated by any man "of woman born." At the end of the play, the rebel army meets Macbeth's forces in a life-or-death struggle.

◆ ◆ ◆

[*Enter* MACBETH, SEYTON, *and* SOLDIERS, *with drum and colors.*]

MACBETH. Hang out our banners on the outward walls.
The cry is still "They come!" Our castle's strength
Will laugh a <u>siege</u> to scorn.

◆ ◆ ◆

Macbeth says that the enemy army will die of famine and disease during the siege.

◆ ◆ ◆

[*A cry within of women.*]
What is that noise?
SEYTON. It is the cry of women, my good lord.

[*Exit.*]

◆ ◆ ◆

Macbeth reflects that, after so much horror in his life, nothing can terrify him.

◆ ◆ ◆

[*Enter* SEYTON.]

30 **MACBETH.** Wherefore[10] was that cry?
SEYTON. The queen, my lord, is dead.
MACBETH. She should[11] have died hereafter;
There would have been a time for such a word.[12]
Tomorrow, and tomorrow, and tomorrow
Creeps in this petty pace from day to day,
35 To the last syllable of recorded time;
And all our yesterdays have lighted fools

Vocabulary Development

siege (SEEJ) *n.* attack or blockade against a fortified place

---

10. **Wherefore** for what; why.
11. **should** inevitably would.
12. **word** message.

The way to dusty death. Out, out, brief
    candle!
Life's but a walking shadow, a poor player
That struts and frets his hour upon the
    stage
40 And then is heard no more. It is a tale
Told by an idiot, full of sound and fury
Signifying nothing.

◆ ◆ ◆

    A messenger arrives to tell Macbeth
that the forest is moving – Birnam Wood is
coming to Dunsinane. It turns out that
Malcolm's soldiers are carrying tree
branches to hide their approach.

    A battle begins. Macduff pursues
Macbeth, eager to face him in single combat.
Macbeth vows he will continue to fight
against the odds, rather than commit suicide.

◆ ◆ ◆

[Enter MACDUFF.]

MACDUFF. Turn, hell-hound, turn!

MACBETH. Of all men else I have avoided
    thee.
But get thee back! My soul is too much
    charged
45 With blood of thine already.[13]

MACDUFF. I have no words:
My voice is in my sword, thou bloodier villain
Than terms[14] can give thee out!

[Fight. Alarum.]

MACBETH. Thou losest labor:
As easy mayst thou the intrenchant[15] air
With thy keen sword impress[16] as make me
    bleed:
50 Let fall thy blade on vulnerable crests;
I bear a charmèd life, which must not yield
To one of woman born.

---

13. **blood . . . already** Macbeth had ordered the murders of Macduff's wife and children.
14. **terms . . . out** words can describe you.
15. **intrenchant** incapable of being cut.
16. **impress** make a dent in.

from **Macbeth** **51**

◆ **Reading Check**

What have "all our
yesterdays" done,
according to Macbeth?
Underline the words that
give the answer.

◆ **Literary Analysis**

In a **Shakespearean tragedy,** a
tragic flaw or weakness leads
the hero to destruction. How
does Macbeth's view of life here
foreshadow his own downfall?

_____

_____

_____

◆ **Reading Check**

Why does Macbeth tell Macduff
to get back?

_____

_____

_____

◆ **Stop to Reflect**

What does Macduff mean when
he says "my voice is in my
sword"?

_____

_____

_____

◆ **Reading Strategy**

In lines 52-55, make a slash mark [/] at the ends of lines where you would pause in **reading verse for meaning.**

◆ **Stop to Reflect**

Why is Macbeth angry now at the witches?

_____

_____

_____

◆ **Vocabulary and Pronunciation**

The accent mark on the underlined word on page 51 shows that *charmèd* is pronounced as two syllables, not one. This pronunciation is used for the sake of the meter, or the rhythm, in Shakespeare's verse. In line 56 on this page, how many syllables are in the pronunciation of *Accursèd*?

_____

◆ **Culture Note**

In England during Shakespeare's time, traveling shows and spectator sports like bear-baiting were common. Why do you think Macduff tells Macbeth that he will become part of a traveling show?

_____

_____

_____

MACDUFF. Despair thy charm,
And let the angel[17] whom thou still hast served
Tell thee, Macduff was from his mother's womb
55 Untimely ripped.[18]
MACBETH. <u>Accursèd</u> be that tongue that tells me so,
For it hath cowed[19] my better part of man![20]
And be these juggling fiends[21] no more believed,
That palter[22] with us in a double sense;
That keep the word of promise to our ear,
60 And break it to our hope. I'll not fight with thee.
MACDUFF. Then yield thee, coward.
And live to be the show and gaze o' th' time;[23]
We'll have thee, as our rarer monsters[24] are,
Painted upon a pole,[25] and underwrit,
65 "Here you may see the tyrant."
MACBETH. I will not yield,
To kiss the ground before young Malcolm's feet,
And to be baited with the rabble's curse.
Though Birnam Wood be come to Dunsinane,[26]
And thou opposed, being of no woman born,
70 Yet I will try the last. Before my body

---

17. **angel** fallen angel; fiend.
18. **his . . . ripped** Macduff's mother died before giving birth to him.
19. **cowed** frightened.
20. **better . . . man** courage.
21. **fiends** the three witches.
22. **palter** juggle.
23. **gaze o' th' time** spectacle of the age.
24. **monsters:** freaks.
25. **Painted . . . pole** pictured on a banner stuck on a pole by a showman's booth.
26. **Birnam . . . Dunsinane** Malcolm's soldiers held tree branches in front of themselves when they marched on Dunsinane, Macbeth's castle.

I throw my warlike shield. Lay on, Macduff;
And damned be him that first cries, "Hold,
    enough!"
            [*Exit, fighting. Alarums.*]
                ◆   ◆   ◆
        Macduff slays Macbeth. In front of the
soldiers, Macduff hails Duncan's son
Malcolm as the new king of Scotland.
                ◆   ◆   ◆
    [*Enter* MACDUFF, *with* MACBETH'S *head.*]
    MACDUFF. Hail, King! For so thou art:
        behold, where stands
    Th' usurper's[27] cursèd head. The time is
        free.[28]
75 I see thee compassed with thy kingdom's
        pearl,[29]
    That speak my <u>salutation</u> in their minds,
    Whose voices I desire aloud with mine:
    Hail, King of Scotland!
    ALL. Hail, King of Scotland!
                ◆   ◆   ◆
        Promising to reward his supporters,
Malcolm invites the army to his coronation.

Literary Analysis

What positive or heroic qualities
does Macbeth as **tragic hero**
display here?

_____

_____

_____

Literary Analysis

How does the conclusion of this
scene in lines 73-78 illustrate the
lively action and vivid spectacle
of **Shakespearean tragedy**?

_____

_____

_____

Vocabulary Development

salutation (sal yoo TAY shuhn) *n.* greeting

---

27. **Th' usurper's . . . head** the head of Macbeth, who had stolen the
throne.
28. **The . . free** Our country is liberated.
29. **compassed . . . pearl** surrounded by the noblest people in the
kingdom.

1. In his speech at lines 3-10, what does Macbeth think he sees?

_____

_____

2. In the spaces below, identify the three things that Macbeth compares human life to in lines 38-42.

   Life is like . . .

   (a) _____

   (b) _____

   (c) _____

3. What does Macduff tell Macbeth that frightens Macbeth and causes him to say that he will not fight Macduff?

_____

_____

4. **Literary Analysis:** In a **Shakespearean tragedy,** the hero's downfall is usually caused by a tragic flaw or weakness. What is Macbeth's tragic flaw, and how does it lead him to disaster?

_____

_____

5. **Reading Strategy:** When you **read verse for meaning,** you follow sentences past line endings.

   (a) How many sentences are there in lines 23-25? _____

   (b) In reading these lines for meaning, where would you pause? Explain.

_____

_____

Writing

Analysis of a Character's Imagination

Shakespeare's tragic heroes combine noble or positive qualities with a tragic flaw, or weakness. For example, Macbeth is a courageous general who is loyal to King Duncan. However, the witches' prophecies lead him to consider betraying his ruler. Urged on by Lady Macbeth, Macbeth yields to his ambition. His first evil deed, the murder of the king, leads to more and more bloodshed.

Throughout the play, Macbeth shows that he is aware of how evil he has become. Write an essay discussing how Macbeth's vivid imagination adds to his own tragedy. Follow these steps as you work on your essay:

1. Identify passages in which Macbeth makes striking comparisons or uses vivid images.

   _____

   _____

2. Find passages where Macbeth seems weary or sorrowful about his own life or life in general.

   _____

   _____

3. Locate the passage in which Macbeth imagines his future if he refuses to fight Macduff. What choice does Macbeth make?

   _____

   _____

4. Write a single sentence to state the main idea of your essay.

   _____

   _____

5. On separate paper, write a draft of your essay. Use quotations and discuss passages that support your main idea.

6. When you have finished your draft, trade papers with a classmate. Offer each other suggestions for revision.

Meditation 17
John Donne

Summary

In 1623, John Donne was the chief religious official at St. Paul's Cathedral in London. After suffering a serious illness, he composed Meditation 17 and similar religious writings. A religious meditation is a thoughtful consideration of matters relating to the church and to God. In Meditation 17, Donne says that the church applies to humanity as a whole. As a result, when he hears a bell tolling for someone about to die, he does not need to ask for whom it is tolling. He imagines that the bell is tolling for him, John Donne, because he is involved with all people. Whether or not the bell tolls specifically for him, it reminds him that he will die and that his only safety lies in God.

Visual Summary

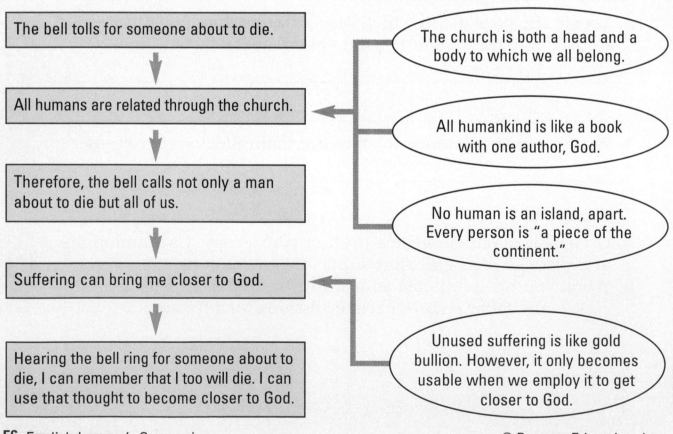

Basic Argument

The bell tolls for someone about to die.

All humans are related through the church.

Therefore, the bell calls not only a man about to die but all of us.

Suffering can bring me closer to God.

Hearing the bell ring for someone about to die, I can remember that I too will die. I can use that thought to become closer to God.

Supporting Comparisons

The church is both a head and a body to which we all belong.

All humankind is like a book with one author, God.

No human is an island, apart. Every person is "a piece of the continent."

Unused suffering is like gold bullion. However, it only becomes usable when we employ it to get closer to God.

LITERARY ANALYSIS

Metaphysical Poetry

Metaphysical poetry is a kind of poetry that is often about philosophy or about the pursuit of wisdom. It uses these devices:
- Conceits, or extended comparisons of things that are unlike
- Paradoxes, or images that seem like contradictions

"Meditation 17" is an essay, but it has many characteristics of metaphysical poetry. For example, in the following passage, John Donne uses a conceit to compare a person to an body of land:

> No man is an island, entire of itself. Every man is a piece of the continent, a part of the main. If a clod be washed away by the sea, Europe is the less, as well as if a promontory were, as well as if a manor of thy friend's or of thine own were.

READING STRATEGY

Recognizing the Speaker's Situation and Motivation

One way to improve your understanding of what you read is to recognize the speaker's situation. Put yourself in the speaker's place. If you are reading an essay that expresses a writer's opinion, try to learn something about the writer's life. The writer's life might give you a clue about what the speaker's motivation is. As you read "Meditation 17," use this chart to help you imagine Donne's situation and his motivation.

Speaker's Words	Situation	Motivation
"When she baptizes a child, that action concerns me; for that child is thereby connected to that head which is my head too."	Donne is a member of the church he is referring to.	He wants to restate how members of the church are joined to one another.

Many words in English have more than one meaning. For example, the word *volume* can refer to a book or to sound levels. It can also refer to the amount of space within a three-dimensional shape. Which meaning is meant here?

_____

Leaves is another multiple-meaning word. It can refer to pages in a book or parts of a green plant. It is also a verb, meaning "goes away." Which meaning is meant here?

_____

Literary Analysis

Here, Donne uses a feature of **metaphysical poetry** when he does an extended comparison of one thing to another, seemingly unrelated thing. This is called a **conceit**. Read the bracketed passage, and then circle the letter of the correct answer.

In this conceit, Donne compares a person to _____.

(a) a foreign language

(b) a chapter in a book

(c) God

(d) a translator

Reading Strategy

Based on Donne's **situation**, what can you guess about his **motivation**?

_____

_____

_____

Meditation 17
John Donne

Donne talks about a bell that is tolling, or ringing. It is announcing someone's death or coming death. He says that maybe the person doesn't know that the bell is tolling for him. He says it might even be for Donne himself, and he doesn't know it. The church that rings the bell is for all people. So are all the things that the church does.

◆　◆　◆

When she baptizes a child, that action concerns me; for that child is thereby connected to that head which is my head too.[1] . . . And when she buries a man, that action concerns me: all mankind is of one author and one <u>volume</u>; when one man dies, one chapter is not torn out of the book, but translated into a better language; and every chapter must be so translated. God employs several translators; some pieces are translated by age, some by sickness, some by war, some by justice; but God's hand is in every translation, and his hand shall bind up all our scattered <u>leaves</u> again for that library where every book shall lie open to one another.

◆　◆　◆

He goes on to say that the bell is not just for the preacher. It is for the people of the church. It is also for Donne, who is suffering from a sickness. . . . The bell tolls for the person who thinks it is tolling for him. If the bell stops for a time, it doesn't matter. The person who thought it was tolling for him is united to God from that moment.

◆　◆　◆

_____

1. **that head which is my head too** In the Bible, St. Paul calls Jesus the head (spiritual leader) of all the faithful.

No man is an island, entire of itself; every man is a piece of the continent, a part of the main.[2] If a clod be washed away by the sea, Europe is the less, as well as if a <u>promontory</u> were, as well as if a <u>manor</u> of thy friend's or of thine own were. Any man's death <u>diminishes</u> me because I am involved in mankind, and therefore never send to know for whom the bell tolls; it tolls for thee.

◆ ◆ ◆

Donne goes on to say that our troubles are good for us. No one has enough of them. Troubles help us mature. They make us fit for God. We might listen to a bell that tolls for someone else and apply its meaning to ourselves. If we do this, we become closer to God, our only security.

Vocabulary Development

promontory (PRAH muhn tor ee) *n.* a high point of land or rock jutting out into a body of water

manor (MAN uhr) *n.* the house of an estate

diminishes (di MIN ish uhs) *v.* lessens, reduces

2. **main** (MAYN) *n.* the mainland.

◆ **English Language Development**

One use of commas is to set off an introductory clause. If you move the clause to the end of the sentence, you don't need the comma. See the chart for an example.

Introductory Clause with Comma	Clause at the End
If the bell stops for a time, it doesn't matter.	It doesn't matter if the bell stops for a time.

Now write your own sentences in the same style. Write one sentence beginning with an introductory clause and a comma. Write the other with the clause at the end.

1. _____

_____

2. _____

_____

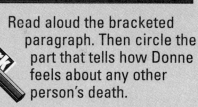

◆ **Read Fluently**

Read aloud the bracketed paragraph. Then circle the part that tells how Donne feels about any other person's death.

1. Put a check by the answer that completes the sentence.

   The tolling bell that Donne hears is announcing. . . .

   ____ a wedding   ____ troubles

   ____ a baptism   ____ a death

2. When Donne says that some people are translated by age, some by sickness, some by war, and some by justice, what does he mean?

   _____

   _____

3. What does Donne mean when he says "No man is an island"?

   _____

   _____

4. **Reading Strategy:** Use clues to help you **determine** what Donne's **situation** is. Based on his situation, what do you think his **motivation** is in writing this essay? Write your answers in this chart.

Donne's Situation	Donne's Motivation

5. **Literary Analysis:** At the end of the essay, Donne talks about troubles. What is the **paradox** that he explains regarding troubles and their role in our lives?

_____

_____

Writing

Persuasive Speech

Use the ideas in "Meditation 17" as the basis for a modern speech. Write a speech that you could deliver today, based on Donne's ideas. Follow these steps:

Prewriting
- List two or three of Donne's arguments.

_____

_____

_____

- List images and comparisons from today that could be used in place of the ones Donne uses.

_____

_____

_____

Drafting
- On separate paper, write an opening sentence with a strong statement or vivid image.
- Now write the first paragraph of your speech. Develop the images and arguments with your modern audience in mind.

Revising
- Read your paragraph out loud. If you hear parts that do not seem to develop your ideas, change them.
- Write a final version of your paragraph.

Presenting
- Share your paragraph with your classmates. Ask for their ideas about how you can expand your paragraph into a short speech.

from Paradise Lost

John Milton

Summary

Paradise Lost is a long narrative poem written from a Christian point of view. It tells how Adam and Eve, the first humans according to Jewish and Christian belief, were tempted by the evil angel Satan to disobey God. This disobedience caused them to lose their home in the garden known as Paradise. Instead of living a life of ease forever, they would have to work and, eventually, die.

In this passage from the beginning of the poem, Milton explains what his subject will be. He also calls on Urania (yoo rā´ nē ə), goddess of astronomy and poetry, to help him write his poem. Then, he tells how Satan, once a great angel, rebelled against God's rule. In punishment, God hurled Satan and the other rebel angels out of heaven. These angels fell to a place of darkness and fire that God prepared for them. As Satan revives after this fall, his lieutenant Beelzebub (bē el´ zə bub´) says that they are defeated. However, Satan is defiant and wants to continue the struggle against God. Satan will seek revenge against God by causing Adam and Eve to lose Paradise.

Visual Summary

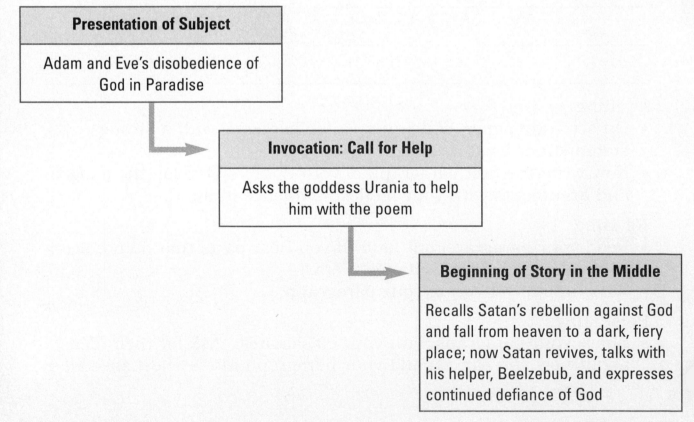

Presentation of Subject
Adam and Eve's disobedience of God in Paradise

Invocation: Call for Help
Asks the goddess Urania to help him with the poem

Beginning of Story in the Middle
Recalls Satan's rebellion against God and fall from heaven to a dark, fiery place; now Satan revives, talks with his helper, Beelzebub, and expresses continued defiance of God

LITERARY ANALYSIS

Epic Poetry

An **epic poem** is a long poem that tells a story about a hero. Epic poems have these features:

- A story that starts in the middle of the action
- A call for divine aid in the telling of the story
- Extended similes, or comparisons using the words *like* or *as*

As you read, look for examples of these features.

READING STRATEGY

Breaking Down Sentences

One way to better understand what you read is to **break down sentences** into smaller parts. Look for the subject and predicate of the main clause. Separate this part from the rest of the sentence. You might want to keep track of sentences you break down in a chart like this:

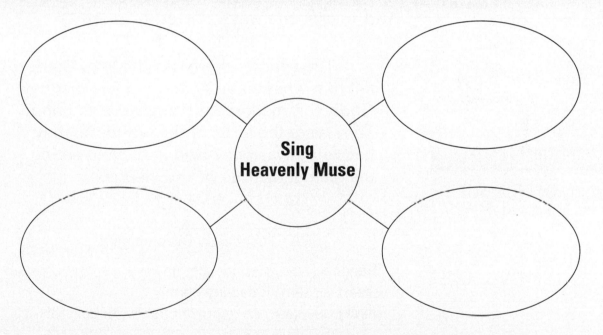

◆ Literary Analysis

In the first paragraph, for whose divine aid does the poet ask in writing his **epic poem?** Circle the answer.

◆ Literary Analysis

What clues tell you that this is an **epic poem?** List two clues.

1. _____

2. _____

◆ Vocabulary and Pronunciation

The words *spirit* and *inspired* have the same root. That root is a Latin word, *spiritus,* that means "breathing, breath, air, life, or soul." Underline the root in each of these words:

inspiration   inspirational

spiritual   spirituality

dispirited   inspiring

◆ Reading Check

What command of God did Adam and Eve disobey?

_____

_____

_____

Of man's first disobedience, and the fruit
Of that forbidden tree, whose mortal[1] taste
Brought death into the world, and all our woe,
With loss of Eden, till one greater Man[2]
Restore us, and regain the blissful seat,
Sing Heavenly Muse,[3]

      ◆   ◆   ◆

    The speaker of the poem suggests that the Muse is the same spirit that inspired Moses. The speaker asks the Muse to help him finish the epic he is now writing. Then the poet asks the Holy Spirit to help him too.

      ◆   ◆   ◆

. . . what in me is dark
Illumine, what is low raise and support;
That to the height of this great argument[4]
I may assert Eternal Providence,
And justify the ways of God to men.

      ◆   ◆   ◆

    The speaker then asks the Holy Spirit to tell him what made Adam and Eve disobey God's commandment. They were so happy. They were the lords of the world. All they had to do was obey God and avoid eating the fruit of the tree of knowledge.

      ◆   ◆   ◆

Vocabulary Development

illumine (i LOO muhn) *v.* light up

assert (uh SERT) *v.* declare firmly

justify (JUS tuh fī) *v.* to prove or show to be right

---

1. **mortal** (MOR tuhl) *adj.* deadly.
2. **one greater Man** Jesus Christ.
3. **Heavenly Muse** (MYOOZ) Urania, the muse of astonomy and sacred poetry in Greek mythology. Here, Milton associates Urania with the holy spirit that inspired Moses. Moses received the Ten Commandments from God. He also wrote the first five books of the Bible, including Genesis, the book on which *Paradise Lost* is based.
4. **argument** (AR gyoo ment) *n.* theme.

Who first seduced them to that foul revolt?
The infernal Serpent; he it was, whose <u>guile</u>
Stirred up with envy and revenge, deceived
The mother of mankind, what time his pride
Had cast him out from Heaven, with all his
  host
Of rebel angels, by whose aid <u>aspiring</u>
To set himself in glory above his peers.

◆ ◆ ◆

The speaker tells more about the fallen angels. Their leader wanted to be equal to God. He waged a war against God. He was very ambitious and fought a brave battle, but he lost. God punished him severely.

◆ ◆ ◆

<u>Him the Almighty Power</u>
<u>Hurled headlong flaming from the ethereal sky</u>
<u>With hideous ruin and combustion down</u>
<u>To bottomless</u> <u>perdition,</u> <u>there to dwell</u>
<u>In adamantine⁵ chains and penal fire.</u>

◆ ◆ ◆

Now Satan is tormented by thoughts of lost <u>happiness</u> and lasting pain. He is in a dungeon full of flames. Yet the flames give off no light. He can never find any <u>peace, rest, or hope</u>. The rebel angels are as far from God and the light of Heaven as possible. Soon Satan sees Beelzebub,⁶ his main helper in the fight against God. He speaks to Beelzebub about how changed Beelzebub is. Once his own brightness outshone that of the other angels. He joined Satan in the fight against

---

Vocabulary Development

guile (GĪL) *n.* deceitful cunning
aspiring (as PĪR ing) *adj.* trying to accomplish a goal
perdition (per DI shun) *n.* complete destruction

---

5. **adamantine** (ad uh MAN teen) *adj.* not able to be broken.
6. **Beelzebub** (bee EL zuh buhb) Usually, this name refers to the chief devil, or Satan. Here, it refers to Satan's main helper among the fallen angels.

from Paradise Lost **65**

◆ **Read Fluently**

Read aloud the bracketed section. Then circle the phrase Milton uses to refer to Satan. Underline the phrase that refers to Eve.

◆ **Reading Strategy**

Break down the difficult underlined **sentence.**

(1) What is the subject (the doer of the action)?

_____

(2) What is the simple predicate (the main verb)?

_____

(3) What is the direct object (the receiver of the action)?

_____

◆ **Vocabulary and Pronunciation**

The suffix *-ness* means "state of, condition, or quality of." Thus, the word *happiness* means "the state of being happy." Write a definition for each of these words:

darkness

_____

brightness

_____

goodness

_____

◆ **English Language Development**

The underlined section shows how commas are used to separate items in a series. Add the necessary commas to each of the following sentences.

Adam and Eve had been happy comfortable and blessed.

Satan was full of pride hate and determination.

Beelzebub calls Satan a prince a chief and a leader of the angels.

◆ Literary Analysis

What details suggest that Satan has the qualities of an **epic hero?** List two.

1. _____

2. _____

◆ Literary Analysis

Epic poems commonly tell of famous battles. What famous battle is Milton writing about?

_____

_____

God, and now misery has joined them both in equal ruin. Satan then tells Beelzebub that he is not sorry for what they did.

◆ ◆ ◆

What though the field be lost?
All is not lost; the unconquerable will
And study of revenge, immortal hate,
And courage never to submit or yield:
And what is else not to be overcome?
That glory never shall his wrath or might
Extort from me.

◆ ◆ ◆

Satan tells Beelzebub that he will never give up in his fight against God. He plans to wage eternal war. Then Beelzebub calls Satan a prince, a chief, and a leader of the angels. He says that the mind and spirit are still strong, even though their glory and happiness have changed to endless misery. Then Beelzebub says that it is clear that God is almighty, for how else could he have won against such a mighty force? He wonders what good it is to have eternal life, if all that is in store for them is eternal punishment. Satan answers Beelzebub:

◆ ◆ ◆

"Fallen cherub, to be weak is miserable,
Doing or suffering:[7] but of this be sure,
To do aught[8] good never will be our task,
But ever to do ill our sole delight,
As being the contrary to his high will
Whom we resist. If then his providence
Out of our evil seek to bring forth good,
Our labor must be to pervert that end,
And out of good still[9] to find means of evil;

◆ ◆ ◆

Vocabulary Development

extort (ex TORT) *v.* to obtain by force

---

7. **doing or suffering:** whether one is active or passive.
8. **aught** (AWT): anything.
9. **still** always.

Satan goes on to say that their activities will cause God grief and trouble. He sees that God has called his good angels back to Heaven. It looks as if the war is over, at least for now. Satan sees this as an opportunity to rest and gather together their overthrown armies. He wants to think about how they can most offend their Enemy in the future. As Satan talks to Beelzebub, he lies chained on a burning lake of fire. His huge body is as big as any monster from ancient stories.

◆ ◆ ◆

So stretched out huge in length the Archfiend
  lay
Chained on the burning lake, nor ever thence
Had risen or heaved his head, but that the will
And high permission of all-ruling Heaven
Left him at large to his own dark <u>designs</u>,
That with <u>reiterated</u> crimes he might
Heap on himself damnation, while he sought
Evil to others, and enraged might see
How all his malice served but to bring forth
Infinite goodness, grace and mercy shown
On man by him seduced, but on himself
Treble confusion, wrath and vengeance poured.

◆ ◆ ◆

Suddenly Satan gets up from the fiery pool. He opens his wings and flies to dry land. Beelzebub follows him. They are both happy to have escaped on their own strength, rather than by the permission of heavenly power.

◆ ◆ ◆

◆ English Language Development

In English, a comma is used to separate a long introductory passage from the rest of the sentence. Add the necessary comma in each of these sentences:

For help in writing his epic Milton turns to the Muse and to the Holy Spirit.

To remain lords of the world Adam and Eve had to obey God's commandment.

Because Satan wanted to be equal to God he waged a war against Him.

◆ Reading Strategy

Break down the bracketed passage into two sentences. Write the sentences below in your own words.

_____

_____

_____

◆ Reading Check

What will Heaven bring out of Satan's evil?

_____

_____

_____

Vocabulary Development

designs (duh ZĪNZ) *n.* plans
reiterated (ree IT er ay tuhd) *v.* repeated

Break down the underlined
sentence. Rewrite it below in
your own words.

_____

_____

_____

The word *hath* is an old-
fashioned way of saying "has."
Here are some other old-
fashioned words:

thee (you)   thy (your)

thine (yours)   thou (you)

Reread the bracketed section. In
what way are these ideas fitting
for the hero of an **epic poem?**

_____

_____

_____

What do you think Satan means
by the underlined comment?

_____

_____

_____

"Is this the region, this the soil, the clime,"
Said then the lost Archangel, "this the seat
That we must change for Heaven, this
    mournful gloom
For that celestial light? Be it so, since he
Who now is sovereign can dispose and bid
What shall be right: farthest from him is best,
<u>Whom reason hath equaled, force hath made
    supreme
Above his equals.</u> Farewell happy fields,
Where joy forever dwells. Hail horrors! Hail
Infernal world! and thou, profoundest Hell
Receive thy new possessor, one who brings
A mind not to be changed by place or time.
The mind is its own place, and in itself
Can make a Heaven of Hell, a Hell of Heaven.
What matter where, if I be still the same,
And what I should be, all but less than he
Whom thunder hath made greater? Here at
    least
We shall be free; the Almighty hath not built
Here for his envy, will not drive us hence:
Here we may reign secure, and in my choice
To reign is worth ambition though in Hell:
<u>Better to reign in Hell than serve in Heaven.</u>"

◆   ◆   ◆

  Satan asks why they should let their
fellow fallen angels lie in the fires. Why not
call them together again? Together, they can
find out what they might regain in Heaven,
or what more they might lose in Hell.

1. Milton asks for help in writing this epic poem. For whose help does he ask?

   _____ and _____

2. What great struggle mentioned in the Bible does Milton describe in this poem?

   _____

3. What is the outcome of the struggle?

   _____

4. What qualities does Satan have in common with an epic hero?

   _____

5. **Literary Analysis:** Put a check in front of each sentence or passage that tells you this is an **epic poem.** You should find four.

   _____ Sing Heavenly Muse

   _____ Then the poet asks the Holy Spirit to help him.

   _____ Their prison is in complete darkness.

   _____ He breaks the silence, speaking to Beelzebub.

   _____ They are both happy to have escaped on their own strength, rather than by the permission of heavenly power.

   _____ Better to reign in Hell than serve in Heaven.

6. **Reading Strategy: Break down** this challenging **sentence** and rewrite it. Put it in the order in which you would say it.

   "What in me is dark illumine, what is low raise and support."

   _____

   _____

Listening and Speaking

Deliver a Speech

Do you think Milton does a good job showing the character of Satan? Prepare a speech in which you answer this question.

- Include your ideas on these points:

1. How well does Milton show Satan's thought processes?

_____

_____

_____

2. How did you respond emotionally to the character of Satan in this poem?

_____

_____

_____

- To support your ideas, use details from the poem.
- Deliver your speech to the class. Ask for feedback from your classmates.

from The Diary
Samuel Pepys

Summary

These excerpts from *The Diary* of Samuel
Pepys (pēps) relate to two disasters that struck
London: the plague of 1664–1665, an outbreak
of disease, and the Great Fire of 1666. Pepys
tells how, during the plague, people risk
spreading the disease by watching the burial
of the dead. However, Pepys and others give
orders to ensure that people no longer do this.
He also hears of a man who lost all but one of
his children to the plague. This man and his
wife shut themselves up in their house to

await death. However, the man gave his one remaining child to a friend so that
this child could escape the disease. Pepys and others in charge agree that the
child can be saved from the man's house.

On the first day of the Great Fire, Pepys views it from the Tower of London. He
hears that it began earlier in the day at a baker's house. Later, he tells the king
and the Duke of York that the only way to stop the fire is to demolish houses
around it. The king tells Pepys to order the Lord Mayor of London to put this
plan into action. Pepys sees numbers of people carrying away their goods to protect them from the fire. The next day, he takes his own valuables to a friend's
house for safekeeping. Then, he returns home.

Visual Summary

Sept. 3, 1665	Sept. 14, 1665	Sept. 2, 1666	Sept. 3, 1666
• confers with others to stop spread of plague • gives orders to prevent people from watching burial of the dead • allows a young child to be rescued from a house infected by plague	• grateful for safety of his valuables and for the general decrease in the numbers of people dying of the plague • depressed by increase of deaths from plague within the city and by the deaths of so many he knows	• views fire from Tower of London • tells king to stop fire by tearing down buildings • king tells him to order the mayor to follow this plan • sees many people taking their valuables from their houses • packs up his own goods	• early in the morning, carries away his own goods to Sir W. Rider's house for safekeeping • feels better that his goods are safe • returns home, but neither he nor his wife can sleep

LITERARY ANALYSIS

Diaries and Journals

A **diary** or **journal** is a daily account of a writer's experiences. It can include . . .

- accounts of a writer's day-to-day activities.
- the writer's comments on local events of the day.
- the writer's comments on worldwide events of the time.

Diaries and journals that become literature can give us personal insights into history. As you read, notice how Pepys's *Diary* gives details of public events.

READING STRATEGY

Drawing Conclusions

When you **draw conclusions,** you use clues to figure out something that might not be stated directly. For example, Pepys mentions that he had his bags of gold ready to carry away. From this detail, you can draw the conclusion that he had some wealth.

As you read, use a chart like this one. On the chart, record details and the conclusions that you draw from them.

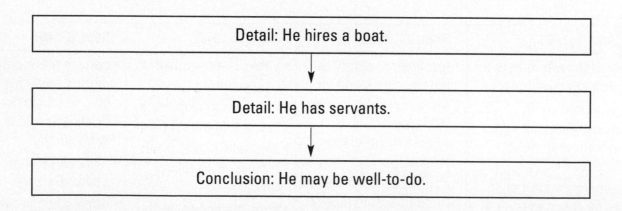

Detail: He hires a boat.

Detail: He has servants.

Conclusion: He may be well-to-do.

from The Diary
Samuel Pepys

On September 3, 1665, Pepys writes a diary entry about the plague.[1] He tells how he has a meeting with six men in the church meeting room. There are a few lords and judges in the group. They want to figure out how to stop the plague. They talk about the madness of some people in London. Even though funeral processions are forbidden, many people still have them. They talk about a man in the town who wanted to save his child.

◆ ◆ ◆

Among other stories, one was very passionate, methought[2] of a complaint brought against a man in the town for taking a child from London from an infected house. Alderman[3] Hooker told us it was the child of a very able citizen in Gracious Street, a saddler,[4] who had buried all the rest of his children of the plague, and himself and wife now being shut up and in despair of escaping, did desire only to save the life of this little child; and so <u>prevailed</u> to have it received stark-naked into the arms of a friend, who brought it (having put it into new fresh clothes) to Greenwich;[5] where upon hearing the story, we did agree it should be permitted to be received and kept in the town.

◆ ◆ ◆

Vocabulary Development

prevailed (pruh VAYLD) *v.* persuaded (someone) to do something

---

1. **the plague** (PLAYG) A plague is any contagious disease that affects many people. Here, it refers to the bubonic plague, which devastated London from 1664 to 1666.
2. **methought** (mee THAWT) an old-fashioned way of saying "I thought."
3. **alderman** (AWL duhr min) a city official ranking just below mayor.
4. **saddler** (SAD ler) *n.* a person who makes, sells, and repairs saddles.
5. **Greenwich** (GREN ich) a section of Greater London.

◆ **Vocabulary and Pronunciation**

In English, the letter *g* can be pronounced like the *g* in *girl* or like the letter *j*, as in *gem*. Write *g* or *j* to tell how the *g* is pronounced in each of these words:

plague _____   judges _____

figure _____   agree _____

raging _____

◆ **Reading Strategy**

What **conclusion** can you **draw** about Pepys's position in his community?

_____

_____

_____

◆ **Vocabulary and Pronunciation**

The letter *u* is sometimes pronounced "yoo," as in *fuel*. It is sometimes pronounced "oo," as in *flu*. Write *yoo* or *oo* to tell how the *u* is pronounced in each of these words:

figure _____   funeral _____

clue _____   endure _____

secured _____

◆ **Reading Strategy**

Based on the story about the baby, what **conclusion** can you **draw** about the general policy toward people who had been exposed to the plague?

_____

_____

_____

In his entry for September 14, 1665, Pepys says that he found some money and plate[6] that he thought he had lost. He also says that the plague seems to be claiming fewer victims.

He goes on to tell of a tavern and an alehouse that have been closed up. The last time he was at the alehouse, someone was dying of the plague there. He says that his waiter has buried a child and is dying himself. A laborer he hired has died of the plague. The boatman whose boat Pepys used every day has also died. Many other people he knows are sick.

◆　◆　◆

To hear that Mr. Lewes hath[7] another daughter sick. And, lastly, that both my servants, W. Hewer and Tom Edwards, have lost their fathers, both in St. Sepulcher's parish, of the plague this week, do put me into great <u>apprehensions</u> of <u>melancholy</u>, and with good reason. But I put off the thoughts of sadness as much as I can, and the rather to keep my wife in good heart and family also.

◆　◆　◆

His entry of September 2, 1666, is about the Great Fire of London. He says that some of his maids see a great fire in the city, so they wake Pepys up. The fire seems to be far off, so he goes back to sleep. In the morning, a maid tells him that more than 300 houses were burned down and the fire is spreading. He walks to the Tower of London and gets up on a high spot. The fire has burned down

Vocabulary Development

apprehensions (ap ree HEN shuns) *n.* fears
melancholy (MEL uhn kohl ee) *v.* sadness

---

6. **plate** (PLAYT) *n.* valuable serving dishes and flatware.
7. **hath** (HATH) an old-fashioned way of saying "has."

◆ **Stop to Reflect**

Do you think Pepys was right to "put off the thoughts of sadness"? Why?

_____

_____

_____

◆ **Reading Check**

What had Pepys been doing when the fire broke out?

_____

_____

_____

St. Magnus's Church and most of Fish Street already. Pepys then takes a boat closer to the fire. He can see people trying to save their goods. Within an hour, the fire is raging in every direction. After the long drought, everything is combustible. Word is brought to the King about the fire.

◆   ◆   ◆

So I was called for, and did tell the King and Duke of York what I saw, and that unless his Majesty did command houses to be pulled down nothing could stop the fire. They seemed much troubled, and the King commanded me to go to my Lord Mayor from him, and command him to spare no houses, but to pull down before the fire every way. The Duke of York bid me tell him that if he would have any more soldiers he shall; and so did my Lord Arlington afterwards, as a great secret.

◆   ◆   ◆

Pepys goes on to describe the streets of London. Everyone is carrying goods that they are trying to save. Then, as the fire progresses, the goods have to be moved again and again. The streets are full of people, horses, and carts carrying goods. Even the boats in the harbor are being filled.

Pepys walks to St. James's Park, where he meets his wife and some friends. They walk to his boat, and they observe the fire from the Thames River. They are as close to the fire as they can get and still avoid the smoke.

◆   ◆   ◆

◆ **Read Fluently**

Read aloud the bracketed section. Underline the part that tells what the King's command was.

◆ **Vocabulary and Pronunciation**

Many words have multiple meanings. For example, *rest* can mean "the remainder" or "to nap." Write a sentence of your own in which you use the underlined word in another meaning.

1. The King said to <u>spare</u> no houses.

_____

_____

2. The <u>fire</u> spread quickly.

_____

_____

3. The flames were not like the <u>fine</u> flames of an ordinary fire.

_____

_____

◆ **Reading Strategy**

What **conclusion** about the fire can you **draw**, based on the way people are moving their belongings?

_____

_____

_____

◆ **Reading Check**

Where did Pepys go after leaving the river? Circle the answer.

◆ **Reading Strategy**

What evidence in this paragraph could lead to the **conclusion** that Pepys was quite wealthy?

_____

_____

_____

◆ **English Language Development**

Compound words are words that are made up of two other words. For example, the word *sun-flower* is made of *sun* and *flower.* For each compound word below, write the two words that it is made of.

highway

_____

alehouse

_____

boatman

_____

firedrops

_____

nightgown

_____

When we could <u>endure</u> no more upon the water, we to a little alehouse on the Bankside, over against the Three Cranes, and there stayed till it was dark almost, and saw the fire grow; and, as it grew darker, appeared more and more, and in corners and upon steeples, and between churches and houses, as far as we could see up the hill of the city, in a most horrid <u>malicious</u> bloody flame, not like the fine flame of an ordinary fire.

◆ ◆ ◆

Pepys goes home "with a sad heart." A friend, Tom Hater, comes over and wants to store some goods at Pepys's house. News comes that the fire is growing. Pepys and his family are forced to start packing up their own goods. By the light of the moon, they carry much of Pepys's goods into the garden. Mr. Hater helps Pepys carry his money and iron chests into the cellar, thinking that is the safest place. Pepys gets his bags of gold ready to carry away. He gets his important papers ready, too. Mr. Hater tries to get some sleep, but he gets very little rest because of all the noise of moving goods out of the house.

◆ ◆ ◆

About four o'clock in the morning, my Lady Batten sent me a cart to carry away all my money, and plate, and best things, to Sir W. Rider's at Bednall Green. Which I did, riding myself in my nightgown in the cart; and, Lord! to see how the streets and the highways are crowded with people running and riding, and

---

Vocabulary Development

endure (en DYOOR) *v.* continue in the same state
malicious (muh LISH uhs) *adj.* with evil intentions

getting of carts at any rate to fetch away things. I find Sir W. Rider tired with being called up all night, and receiving things from several friends. His house full of goods, and much of Sir W. Baten's and Sir W. Pen's. I am eased at my heart to have my treasure so well secured. Then home, with much ado to find a way, nor any sleep all this night to me nor my poor wife.

1. According to the entry for September 3, 1665, how did the saddler try to save his only surviving child?

_____

2. Put a check in front of the five words that could describe Pepys.

____ curious   ____ well-to-do

____ foolish   ____ mean-spirited

____ observant   ____ sympathetic

____ helpful   ____ poor

3. (a) What does Pepys recommend to the King when the fire is raging?

_____

    (b) Do you think this is good advice? Answer yes or no. _____

Explain your answer.

_____

_____

4. **Literary Analysis:** Pepys's *Diary* makes the plague and the Great Fire seem real to modern readers. What qualities does the **diary** have that make it more interesting than a mere historical account? Name two, and explain your answers.

    1. _____

    _____

    2. _____

    _____

5. **Reading Strategy:** Based on Pepys's account of the Great Fire, what **conclusions** can you **draw** about how well London was prepared for fires? List two.

1. _____

2. _____

Listening and Speaking

Performance as a Town Crier

In the seventeenth century, town criers called out news in the streets. Plan a **performance as a town crier,** calling out news during the plague or the fire. Follow these steps:
- Use the library to find out how town criers performed their jobs.
- Apply what you learn to come up with the best gestures and vocal styles for the job.
- Get information from Pepys's *Diary* about what kind of news would be reported.
- Plan what you will say during your performance.
- Present your performance to your class.
- After your performance, share your thoughts about this early way of spreading news.

from Gulliver's Travels

Jonathan Swift

Summary

The novel *Gulliver's Travels* describes four imaginary voyages of Lemuel Gulliver, the narrator. Swift uses these voyages to satirize, or humorously criticize, the customs and institutions of his time. The first voyage takes Gulliver to Lilliput (lil′ ə put′), the kingdom of the six-inch-tall Lilliputians (lil′ ə pyo͞o′ shənz).

This excerpt begins during a discussion between Gulliver and a Lilliputian official concerning the affairs of the Lilliputian empire. The official tells him about a conflict within Lilliput about whether to break eggs from the little end or the big end. The same disagreement caused a war between Lilliput and a country named Blefuscu. (Swift uses the dispute concerning eggs to satirize religious disputes between Protestants and Catholics. Lilliput stands for England, and Blefuscu represents France.) Gulliver then helps the Lilliputians by wading and swimming out to Blefuscu's fleet, seizing it, and bringing it back to Lilliput. The Emperor of Lilliput wants to enslave the people of Blefuscu, but Gulliver argues against this idea. However, this argument causes some officials to plot against him.

Visual Summary

Purpose	Details to Achieve This Purpose
• To criticize and make fun of religious disputes between Protestants and Catholics within England • To criticize and make fun of religious disputes between Protestant England and Catholic France	• There have been disputes within Lilliput over whether to break an egg at the little end (this belief represents Protestantism) or at the big end (this belief represents Catholicism). • There is a war between Lilliput (representing England) and Blefuscu (representing France).
• To criticize and make fun of power-hungry rulers in Europe	• Gulliver seizes Blefuscu's fleet. • The Emperor of Lilliput rejoices and wants to enslave the people of Blefuscu. • Gulliver argues with the Emperor, stating that he will never help to enslave a free people.

LITERARY ANALYSIS

Satire

Satire is writing that uses humor to poke fun at human error and foolishness. Satire can be good-humored, or it can be bitter.

Writers of satire usually don't name their targets. Instead, they make up imaginary characters and situations to mask their targets. Swift uses masks like these:

- Imaginary lands, like Lilliput, the land of the little people
- Made-up characters, like the Lilliputians and their enemies, the Blefuscudians
- Fictional conflicts, like that between the Big-Endians and the Little-Endians

Satirists often use **irony,** a contradiction between the actual meaning of the words and the meaning intended by the writer. As you read, use this chart to help you understand Swift's use of irony.

What Swift Says	What He Means
"Many . . . volumes have been published" about the best way to break an egg.	People often argue too much about unimportant things.

READING STRATEGY

Interpreting

You won't get the point a satirist is trying to make if you fail to interpret the masks used to hint at their true targets. To **interpret,** or figure out, a satire, follow these tips:

- Read the background before you begin reading the selection.
- Read footnotes as you go along.
- Recognize and figure out ironic meanings.

In English, the letter *w* can be either silent, as in *wrinkle,* or voiced, as in *way.* Write *silent* or *voiced* to tell how the *w* is pronounced in each of these words:

shipwreck _____

war _____

write _____

wakes _____

wades _____

wrong _____

◆ **Reading Strategy**

How does the footnote help you **interpret** Swift's satire?

_____

_____

◆ **Literary Analysis**

Swift says that Lilliput and Blefuscu cannot agree on the correct way of breaking eggs. Why do you think he makes this the cause of the conflict between the two countries in his **satire?**

_____

_____

from Gulliver's Travels
Jonathan Swift

Lemuel Gulliver, the narrator, is a doctor on a ship. When he survives a shipwreck, he swims to shore. There, he drifts off to sleep. When he wakes up, he finds that he has been tied down by the Lilliputians. These people are only six inches tall. After a time, Gulliver becomes friendly with the little people. He listens to conversations in the Lilliputian court that remind him of English affairs of state. One day, he talks with the Lilliputian Principal Secretary of Private Affairs. He tells Gulliver that they are at war with the island of Blefuscu.[1] The two countries have been at war for the past three years.

◆ ◆ ◆

It is <u>allowed</u> on all hands, that the primitive way of breaking eggs before we eat them, was upon the larger end; but his present Majesty's grandfather, while he was a boy, going to eat an egg, and breaking it according to the ancient practice, happened to cut one of his fingers. Whereupon the Emperor, his father, published an <u>edict</u>, commanding all his subjects, upon great penalties, to break the smaller end of their eggs. The people so highly resented this law that our histories tell us there have been six rebellions raised on that account; wherein one emperor lost his life, and another his crown.[2]

◆ ◆ ◆

Vocabulary Development

allowed (uh LOWD) *v.* thought

edict (EE dikt) *n.* an official public announcement having the force of law

---

1. **Blefuscu** stands for France.
2. **It is allowed . . . crown** Here, Swift is satirizing the arguments in England between the Catholics (Big-Endians) and the Protestants (Little-Endians). King Henry VIII, who "broke" with the Catholic Church is referred to. So is King Charles I, who "lost his life." And so is King James, who lost his "crown."

The Secretary tells Gulliver that Blefuscu constantly starts these rebellions. He says that eleven thousand persons have died rather than agree to break their eggs at the smaller end.

◆ ◆ ◆

Many hundred large volumes have been published upon this controversy; but the books of the Big-Endians have been long forbidden, and the whole party rendered incapable by law of holding employments.[3]

◆ ◆ ◆

The Secretary then says that the Blefuscudians make accusations against the Lilliputians. They say that the Lilliputians go against an important religious teaching of the great prophet Lustrog. The Secretary then explains the Lilliputians' view.

◆ ◆ ◆

This, however, is thought to be a mere strain upon the text, for the words are these: That all true believers shall break their eggs at the convenient end; and which is the convenient end, seems, in my humble opinion, to be left to every man's conscience, or at least in the power of the chief magistrate[4] to determine.

◆ ◆ ◆

The Secretary then says that the Blefuscudians are preparing to attack with a fleet of fifty war ships. Gulliver says that he will defend Lilliput against all invaders.

A channel 800 yards wide separates the two kingdoms. At high tide, it is about six feet deep. Gulliver orders the strongest cable and iron bars available. The cable is about as thick as thread, and the iron bars are like knitting needles. He triples the cable to make it stronger. He twists three iron bars together to make hooks.

---

3. **holding employments** holding office. (The Test Act of 1673 prevented Catholics from holding public office.)
4. **chief magistrate** (CHEEF MAJ uh strayt): ruler.

Do you think the cause of breaking eggs at the smaller end is worth dying for? Write *yes* or *no,* and explain your answer.

_____

_____

_____

◆ **Reading Strategy**

In this paragraph, Swift is satirizing people who hate other people because of religious differences. Circle two phrases that clearly support this **interpretation.**

◆ **English Language Development**

In English, there are two ways to show comparisons of adjectives and adverbs. We can add *-er* and *-est* to show comparative and superlative degrees, as in *bigger* and *biggest.* Or we can use the words *more* and *most,* as in *more beautiful* and *most beautiful.* Generally, an adjective or adverb of three or more syllables uses *more* and *most* for comparisons. Also, any adverb that ends in *-ly* uses *more* and *most.* Complete the following chart by adding comparative and superlative forms of the words in column 1.

Positive Degree	Comparative Degree	Superlative Degree
Example: strong	*stronger*	*strongest*
tall		
primitive		
highly		
frightened		
great		

Here, Gulliver uses his glasses as a shield in a military operation. What is ironic about this **satire?**

_____

_____

Gulliver wades into the channel and fastens a hook to each of the fifty ships. He holds them all together with cable. Then he cuts the cables that hold the anchors. As he does all this, the enemy shoots thousands of tiny arrows at him. Luckily, his eyes are protected by his glasses. Gulliver wades across the channel with the ships. When he gets to shore, he is made a *Nardac* on the spot. This is the highest title of honor in Lilliput.

◆　◆　◆

His Majesty desired I would take some other opportunity of bringing all the rest of his enemy's ships into his ports. And so unmeasurable is the ambition of princes, that he seemed to think of nothing less than reducing the whole empire of Blefuscu into a province and governing it by a viceroy; of destroying the Big-Endian exiles and compelling that people to break the smaller end of their eggs, by which he would remain sole monarch of the whole world.

◆　◆　◆

What does Gulliver say that causes the Emperor to turn against him?

_____

_____

_____

Gulliver thinks this is wrong. He says that he would never help to bring free and brave people into slavery. From then on, there is a campaign against Gulliver. Gulliver comments:

◆　◆　◆

Of so little weight are the greatest services to princes when put into the balance with a refusal to gratify their passions.

1. Describe the conflict between Big-Endians and Little-Endians over the breaking of eggs.

_____

_____

2. What is the most important physical difference between the Lilliputians and Gulliver?

_____

_____

3. What does the size of the Lilliputians suggest about how Swift regards the importance of their conflict?

_____

_____

4. Complete this chart to show three targets of Swift's satire. In column 1, tell what happens in the text. In column 2, tell what Swift is satirizing.

What Happens in the Text	What Swift Is Satirizing
1.	
2.	
3.	

5. **Literary Analysis:** Put a check in front of each example that tells you this is an **satire**.

_____ Lemuel Gulliver works as a doctor on a ship.

_____ The Lilliputians and the Blefuscudians have wars over how to break an egg.

_____ The Blefuscudians have 50 war ships.

_____ Eleven thousand people died rather than break their eggs a different way.

_____ The Secretary believes that the proper way to break eggs should be left to a person's conscience.

_____ The Emperor of Lilliput wants to make Blefuscu a province of Lilliput.

6. **Reading Strategy:** Why is it necessary to **interpret** a satire like *Gulliver's Travels*?

_____

_____

Writing

Satirical Paragraph

In his novel, Swift uses irony and fantasy to make fun of human vices and foolishness. Write your own satirical paragraph that makes fun of a foolish behavior or trend in today's world.

Prewriting Choose a particular behavior, trend, or attitude to attack. Then, on separate paper, list things its supporters might say to defend this behavior.

Drafting Refer to your notes as you write your paragraph. Use the most outrageous argument for the behavior, trend, or attitude you are satirizing. Make this argument the opening of your paragraph as you pretend to support what you are attacking. Continuing by writing more support in a way that seems positive but is really ridiculous.

Revising Read your paragraph aloud to a partner. If parts of it fall flat, look for ways to improve your satire with irony.

Lines Composed a Few Miles Above Tintern Abbey

William Wordsworth

Summary

This poem was written in 1798 during Words-worth's second visit to the valley of the River Wye and the ruins of Tintern Abbey in Wales. The abbey was once a great medieval church. Wordsworth had passed through the region alone five years earlier, but this time he brought his sister with him to share the experience.

In the poem, he describes the scene as it appears to him on this second visit. Then, he tells how memories of his first visit comforted him amid the noise of towns and cities. He no longer feels as passionate about nature as he did five years earlier. However, he now has a sense of a "spirit" in nature that "rolls through all things." Also, he is glad to be here with his dear sister. He sees in her eyes his "former pleasures" in nature, and he calls on the moon and the winds to bless her. Finally, he looks ahead and imagines her as older and perhaps experiencing "solitude. . . fear. . . pain, or grief." He hopes that she will be healed when she remembers him and this time they spent together.

Visual Summary

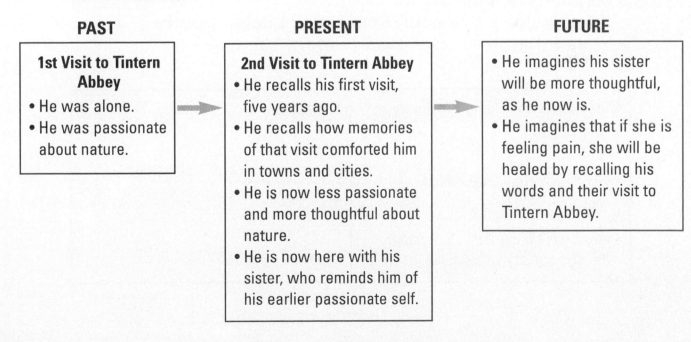

PAST	PRESENT	FUTURE
1st Visit to Tintern Abbey • He was alone. • He was passionate about nature.	**2nd Visit to Tintern Abbey** • He recalls his first visit, five years ago. • He recalls how memories of that visit comforted him in towns and cities. • He is now less passionate and more thoughtful about nature. • He is now here with his sister, who reminds him of his earlier passionate self.	• He imagines his sister will be more thoughtful, as he now is. • He imagines that if she is feeling pain, she will be healed by recalling his words and their visit to Tintern Abbey.

LITERARY ANALYSIS

Romanticism and the Lyric

Romanticism is the name for a movement in the arts that swept over Europe in the late eighteenth century. The works of many Romantic poets include these elements:
- Simplicity or directness of language
- The expression of intense, spontaneous feelings
- Deeply felt responses to nature

English Romantic writers wrote from the heart. The **lyric poem** is well suited to their vision and ideals. A lyric poem is a poem in which a single speaker expresses personal emotions and observations.

READING STRATEGY

Using Literary Context

Literary context is the overall group of literary practices and assumptions that influence a writer during his or her career. Together with the work of his fellow Romantics, Wordsworth's new style of writing poetry shaped the attitudes of several generations of other poets.

Use this chart to identify details and qualities in the selection that were revolutionary at the time.

Characteristic of Romantic Poetry	Example
• a love of nature	
• emphasis on feelings rather than reason	
• emphasis on the individual rather than on society as a whole	

Lines Composed a Few Miles Above Tintern Abbey
William Wordsworth

Five years have passed since Wordsworth last visited the valley of the River Wye and the ruins of Tintern Abbey in Wales. On a second visit, he has brought his sister Dorothy with him to share the experience.

◆ ◆ ◆

Five years have passed; five summers, with
  the length
Of five long winters! and again I hear
These waters, rolling from their mountain
  springs
With a soft inland murmur. Once again
5 Do I <u>behold</u> these steep and lofty cliffs,
That on a wild <u>secluded</u> scene impress
Thoughts of more deep seclusion; and
  connect
The landscape with the quiet of the sky.

◆ ◆ ◆

The poet lies under a sycamore tree. He observes the silent, peaceful orchards and farms around him.

◆ ◆ ◆

These beauteous[1] forms,
10 Through a long absence, have not been to me
As is a landscape to a blind man's eye:
But oft,[2] in lonely rooms, and 'mid the <u>din</u>
Of towns and cities, I have owed to them
In hours of weariness, sensations sweet,
15 Felt in the blood, and felt along the heart.

◆ ◆ ◆

Vocabulary Development

behold (bee HOHLD) *v.* see
secluded (suh KLOOD uhd) *adj.* isolated
din (DIN) *n.* loud noise

---

1. **beauteous** (BYOO tee uhs) *adj.* beautiful.
2. **oft** *adv.* often.

Lines Composed a Few Miles Above Tintern Abbey **89**

◆ Vocabulary and Pronunciation

In English, the suffixes *–sion* and *–tion* often mean "the state of." If the adjective *secluded* in line 6 means "isolated" or "hidden away," what does the noun *seclusion* mean?

_____

_____

◆ Reading Check

Mark the Text

In the bracketed passage, circle two features of the scene that the speaker notices with his senses of hearing and vision.

◆ English Language Development

An apostrophe may either show possession, as in the phrase *the poet's sister,* or it may stand for a missing letter. The word *'mid* is short for *amid,* meaning "in the middle of." What letters do you think are missing in the word *o'clock,* used to tell time?

_____

_____

◆ Stop to Reflect

Mark the Text

Reread lines 13-15 and underline the answers to these questions.

(1) Where was the speaker located when he felt "sensations sweet"?

(2) In what parts of his body did he have these feelings?

Memories of peaceful nature are precious to the poet. They make him a kinder, better person. They also inspire his soul. In moments of distress, memories of the Wye valley have consoled his spirit.

◆ ◆ ◆

And now, with gleams of half-extinguished[3]
   thought,
With many recognitions dim and faint,
And somewhat[4] of a sad <u>perplexity</u>,
The picture of the mind revives again;
20 While here I stand, not only with the sense
Of present pleasure, but with pleasing
   thoughts
That in this moment there is life and food
For future years.

◆ ◆ ◆

The speaker remembers how he felt about nature on his first visit five years ago. Then he was younger and more passionate. Now he is more mature and reflective.

◆ ◆ ◆

For I have learned
To look on nature, not as in the hour
25 Of thoughtless youth; but hearing
   oftentimes
The still, sad music of humanity,
Nor harsh nor <u>grating</u>, though of ample
   power
To chasten[5] and subdue. And I have felt
A presence that disturbs me with the joy

◆ **Read Fluently**

Read the bracketed passage aloud. How does the speaker relate the present to the future in this passage?

_____

_____

_____

◆ **Reading Check**

What has caused the speaker to look differently at nature?

_____

_____

_____

_____

Vocabulary Development

perplexity (puhr PLEK suh tee) *n.* confusion; bewilderment
grating (GRAYT ing) *adj.* annoying; irritating

---

3. **half-extinguished** *adj.* half-destroyed.
4. **somewhat** *adv.* something.
5. **chasten** (CHAY suhn) *v.* punish in order to correct.

30 Of <u>elevated</u> thoughts; a sense <u>sublime</u>
    Of something far more deeply interfused,[6]
    Whose dwelling is the light of setting suns,
    And the round ocean and the living air,
    And the blue sky, and in the mind of man;
35 <u>A motion and a spirit, that impels</u>
    <u>All thinking things, all objects of all</u>
        <u>thought,</u>
    <u>And rolls through all things.</u> Therefore am I
        still
    A lover of the meadows and the woods
    And mountains; and of all that we behold
40 From this green earth; of all the mighty
        world
    Of eye, and ear—both what they half create
    And what perceive; well pleased to
        recognize
    In nature and the language of the sense,
    The anchor of my purest thoughts, the
        nurse,
45 The guide, the guardian of my heart, and
        soul
    Of all my moral being.

                ◆   ◆   ◆

        The speaker prays that his sister will
    also experience the joy that nature offers.
    The quietness and beauty of nature have the
    power to comfort us in all the troubles of life.
    The poet predicts that his sister will cherish
    precious memories of their visit together.

                ◆   ◆   ◆

◆ Literary Analysis

In **Romanticism**, a deeply felt
response to nature is an
important theme. In the
underlined passage, what
feeling about all creation does
nature inspire in the speaker?

_____

_____

_____

◆ Reading Strategy

Literary context is the group of
assumptions that influence a
writer. How do the bracketed
lines reflect the literary context
of Romanticism?

_____

_____

_____

Vocabulary Development

elevated (EL uh vay tuhd) *adj.* noble; inspiring
sublime (suh BLĪM) *adj.* noble and thrilling; majestic
impels (im PELZ) *v.* pushes; moves forward

---

6. **interfused** (in tuhr FYOOZD) *adj.* closely linked together.

In line 50, the words *wilt thou* are archaic or old-fashioned forms meaning "will you." Identify another archaic word in line 53.

_____

_____

According to the speaker, what are the two reasons that the woods and cliffs have become "more dear" to him?

Reason 1:

_____

_____

Reason 2:

_____

_____

Nor, perchance—
If I should be where I no more can hear
Thy voice, nor catch from thy wild eyes
   these gleams
50 Of past existence—wilt thou then forget
That on the banks of this delightful stream
We stood together; and that I, so long
A worshipper of Nature, hither came
Unwearied in that service: rather say
55 With warmer love—oh! with far deeper zeal
Of holier love. Nor wilt thou then forget,
That after many wanderings, many years
Of absence, these steep woods and lofty
   cliffs,
60 And this green <u>pastoral</u> landscape, were to
   me
More dear, both for themselves and for thy
   sake!

Vocabulary Development

pastoral (PAS tuh ruhl) *adj.* rural

---

1. How long has it been since the poet last visited Tintern Abbey?

   _____

   _____

2. How have the poet's memories of his first visit helped him?

   _____

   _____

3. Explain the difference in the poet's attitude on his first and second visit to Tintern Abbey. Use the chart below.

First Visit	Second Visit

4. What wish for his sister does the poet express toward the end of the poem?

   _____

   _____

5. **Literary Analysis:** In a **Romantic lyric poem**, the speaker often expresses intense, personal feelings. A second feature of Romantic lyric poems is a deep response to nature. Identify a specific passage of the poem that illustrates both of these characteristics.

   _____

   _____

6. **Reading Strategy:** The **literary context** of a period is the group of attitudes that influence a writer. Imagine that you are a sociable, city-dwelling writer. Your polished verse is directed to the minds of readers, rather than their hearts. Explain how you might react to lines 9-15 of "Tintern Abbey."

_____

_____

Listening and Speaking

A Photo Essay Presentation

A **photo essay** uses a carefully arranged series of pictures to tell a story or illustrate a theme. In a photo essay, brief captions under or next to each picture identify the subject. The captions may also relate the pictures to the overall narrative or theme.

During the late eighteenth and early nineteenth century, Romanticism affected painting and music as well as literature. Painters, for example, chose intensely dramatic or emotional subjects.

- With a small group of classmates, research Romanticism in painting.
- Then assemble a photo essay presentation. The list below shows some Romantic painters whose work you may explore:

  John Constable
  J. M. W. Turner
  Eugène Delacroix
  Caspar David Friedrich
  Thomas Cole

- Share your photo essay in an oral presentation, such as a slide show or a PowerPoint presentation. In your presentation, use informal expressions for liveliness and technical language for precision.

The Rime of the Ancient Mariner
Samuel Taylor Coleridge

Summary

An ancient Mariner, or old sailor, stops a guest on his way to a wedding. He tells the Wedding Guest about a voyage through strange seas. On this voyage, the Mariner killed a sea bird known as an Albatross. As a result, a curse fell on the ship and the whole crew died, except for the Mariner. He began to find forgiveness only when he blessed the water snakes he saw near the ship. After further adventures, he returned home. Now, to make up for his evil deed, he must wander the world telling his story. The Mariner concludes by telling the Wedding Guest to love "All things both great and small." After hearing the Mariner's tale, the Wedding Guest is "A sadder and a wiser man."

Visual Summary

Exposition	Rising Action	Climax	Falling Action	Resolution
• Mariner stops Wedding Guest to tell his story	• in story, Mariner's ship sailed toward south pole • Mariner killed an Albatross • ship sailed into "silent sea" and crew were thirsty • crew hung the Albatross around Mariner's neck • evil ship approached and crew died • Mariner was unable to pray	• watching water snakes, Mariner blessed them in his heart • Mariner could pray and Albatross dropped from his neck	• spirits possessed bodies of crew to sail the ship • Mariner fainted and heard two spirit voices discussing him • Mariner sailed home and asked a blessing of a holy man	• Mariner must wander the earth telling his tale • Mariner tells Wedding Guest to love "All things both great and small" • Wedding Guest who hears the tale is "A sadder and a wiser man"

LITERARY ANALYSIS
Poetic Sound Devices

Poetic sound devices give Romantic poetry some of its beauty and emotional effect. Here are examples of some of these sound effects.

- **Alliteration** is the repetition of a consonant sound at the beginnings of words: "The Wedding Guest <u>st</u>ood <u>st</u>ill."
- **Internal rhyme** is the use of rhymes within a poetic line: "The guests are m<u>et</u>, the feast is s<u>et</u> . . ."
- **Assonance** is the repetition of a vowel sound in stressed syllables that have different consonant sounds: "Wh<u>i</u>les all the n<u>i</u>ght, through fog-smoke wh<u>i</u>te, / Glimmered the wh<u>i</u>te Moonsh<u>i</u>ne."
- **Consonance** is the repetition of similar final consonant sounds in stressed syllables with different vowel sounds: "And a good south w<u>ind</u> sprung up beh<u>ind</u> . . ."

READING STRATEGY
Analyzing Poetic Effects

Analyzing poetic effects, such as sound devices, will help you appreciate poetry. As you read, use this chart. Find examples of alliteration, internal rhyme, assonance, and consonance. Then identify their effects.

Passage	Sound Device	Image	Effect of Sound on Image
"Whiles all the night, through fog-smoke white,/ Glimmered the white Moonshine."	1. **Internal rhyme:** night / white 2. **Assonance:** whiles / night / white / Moonshine	Ship and sea in fog on a moonlit night	1. Rhyme suggests sameness of scene and blurring of vision. 2. Assonance suggests the eeriness of the scene.

The Rime of the Ancient Mariner
Samuel Taylor Coleridge

It is an ancient Mariner,
And he stoppeth one of three.
"By thy long gray beard and glittering eye,
Now wherefore stopp'st thou me?"

5 "The Bridegroom's doors are opened wide,
And I am next of kin;
The guests are met, the feast is set:
May'st hear the merry din."

He holds him with his skinny hand,
10 "There was a ship," quoth[1] he.
"Hold off! unhand[2] me, graybeard loon!"
Eftsoons[3] his hand dropped he.

He holds him with his glittering eye—
The Wedding Guest stood still,
15 And listens like a three years' child:
The Mariner hath his will.

◆ ◆ ◆

The mariner tells how his ship sails
south until it crosses the equator. A storm
then drives the ship to the South Pole.

◆ ◆ ◆

"The ice was here, the ice was there,
The ice was all around;
It cracked and growled, and roared and
    howled,
20 Like noises in a swound!"[4]

1. **quoth** (KWOHTH) *v.* said.
2. **unhand** *v.* release.
3. **Eftsoons** *adv.* immediately.
4. **swound** *n.* swoon; fainting spell.

◆ Reading Check

Circle two phrases in the first stanza that describe the mariner.

◆ Vocabulary and Pronunciation

An **idiom** is an expression that is unique to a particular language. If *kin* means "blood relative," what does the idiom *next of kin* mean?

_____

_____

_____

◆ Stop to Reflect

Underline the line in the bracketed stanza that explains how the mariner is able to make the wedding guest listen to his story.

Mark the Text

◆ Literary Analysis

Which line in this stanza contains an example of **internal rhyme**? Circle the rhyming words.

"At length did cross an Albatross,
Thorough[5] the fog it came;
As if it had been a Christian soul,
We hailed it in God's name.

25 "It ate the food it ne'er had eat,[6]
And round and round it flew.
The ice did split with a thunder-fit;
The <u>helmsman</u> steered us through!

"And a good south wind sprung up behind;
30 The Albatross did follow,
And every day, for food or play,
Came to the mariner's hollo!

◆ English Language Development

An apostrophe may indicate possession, as in the phrase *the ship's crew.* An apostrophe may also indicate a missing letter. What letter is missing in *ne'er*?

_____

"In mist or cloud, on mast or shroud,[7]
It perched for vespers[8] nine;
35 Whiles all the night, through fog-smoke white,
Glimmered the white Moonshine."

"God save thee, ancient Mariner!
From the <u>fiends</u>, that plague thee thus!—
Why look'st thou so?"[9] "With my crossbow
40 I shot the Albatross!"

◆ ◆ ◆

◆ Stop to Reflect

In the bracketed lines, what events does the speaker seem to link to the presence of the albatross around the ship?

_____

_____

_____

The breeze drops and the ship is becalmed. The crew runs out of water. The mariner's shipmates condemn him for killing the albatross.

◆ ◆ ◆

◆ Reading Check

There are two speakers in the underlined stanza. Who speaks which lines?

_____

_____

Vocabulary Development

helmsman (HELMZ muhn) *n.* steersman of a ship
fiends (FEENDZ) *n.* devils

---

5. **thorough** *prep.* through.
6. **eat** (ET) old form of *eaten.*
7. **shroud** (SHROWD) *n.* ropes stretching from the ship's side to the masthead.
8. **vespers** *n.* evenings.
9. **God . . . so** spoken by the Wedding Guest.

"Ah, well a-day! What evil looks
Had I from old and young!
Instead of the cross, the Albatross
About my neck was hung!"

◆ ◆ ◆

A mysterious, ghostly ship approaches.
Aboard the ship are Death and his mate, the
lady Life-in-Death. The mariner's shipmates
die, one by one.

◆ ◆ ◆

45 "One after one, by the star-dogged Moon,[10]
Too quick for groan or sigh,
Each turned his face with a <u>ghastly</u> pang,
And cursed me with his eye.

"Four times fifty living men,
50 (And I heard nor sigh nor groan)
<u>With heavy thump, a lifeless lump,
They dropped down one by one.</u>

"The souls did from their bodies fly—
They fled to <u>bliss</u> or woe!
55 And every soul, it passed me by,
Like the whizz of my crossbow!"

◆ ◆ ◆

The mariner realizes he is cursed. He
suffers spiritual torture. He is the only one
alive on the ship. He tries to pray, but he
cannot.

◆ ◆ ◆

Vocabulary Development

ghastly (GAST lee) _adj._ horrible
bliss (BLIS) _n._ great joy or happiness

---

10. **star-dogged Moon** omen of impending evil to sailors.

© Pearson Education, Inc.

The Rime of the Ancient Mariner **99**

(1) Which words in the underlined section illustrate **assonance?**

_____

_____

_____

(2) Which words illustrate **alliteration?**

_____

_____

_____

(3) What mood does the vivid description in these lines create?

_____

_____

_____

Read the bracketed stanza aloud. What do you think may be the symbolic significance of the albatross finally dropping from the mariner's neck into the sea? (*Hint:* What does the mariner do just beforehand?)

_____

_____

_____

"Beyond the shadow of the ship,
I watched the water snakes:
They moved in tracks of shining white,
60   And when they reared, the elfish[11] light
Fell off in hoary[12] flakes.

"Within the shadow of the ship
I watched their rich <u>attire:</u>
<u>Blue, glossy green, and velvet black,</u>
65   <u>They coiled and swam; and every track</u>
<u>Was a flash of golden fire.</u>

"O happy living things! no tongue
Their beauty might declare:
A spring of love gushed from my heart,
70   And I blessed them unaware:
Sure my kind saint took pity on me,
And I blessed them unaware.

"The selfsame moment I could pray;
And from my neck so free
75   The Albatross fell off, and sank
Like lead into the sea."

◆ ◆ ◆

The spirits of angels guide the ship onward. Two spirits discuss the mariner's crime of killing the harmless albatross. The mariner's suffering and prayers break the spell of the curse. He returns to his native country. A saintly hermit absolves the mariner from sin. Ever since his journey, the mariner must tell his tale to listeners like the wedding guest. He bids the guest farewell.

◆ ◆ ◆

Vocabulary Development

attire (uh TĪR) *n.*   fine clothing

---

11. **elfish** *adj.* like an elf, or mischievous spirit.
12. **hoary** *adj.* white.

"Farewell, farewell! but this I tell
To thee, thou Wedding Guest!
He prayeth well, who loveth well
80 Both man and bird and beast.

"He prayeth best, who loveth best
All things both great and small:
For the dear God who loveth us,
He made and loveth all."

85 The Mariner, whose eye is bright,
Whose beard with age is hoar,
Is gone; and now the Wedding Guest
Turned from the bridegroom's door.

He went like one that hath been stunned
90 And is of sense forlorn;
A sadder and a wiser man,
He rose the morrow morn.

◆ Reading Check

According to the mariner, what kind of person prays well? Underline the words in this stanza that give the answer.

◆ Stop to Reflect

(1) Why do you think the wedding guest is sadder?

_____

_____

_____

(2) Why is he wiser?

_____

_____

_____

1. On what occasion does the ancient mariner tell his story?

_____

2. Why does the mariner wear the albatross around his neck?

_____

3. Why does the albatross finally fall from the mariner's neck?

_____

4. What larger lesson about human life might this story suggest?

_____

5. **Literary Analysis:** Coleridge uses **poetic sound devices** to achieve emotional effects in "The Ancient Mariner." What two sound devices does he use in the line "It cracked and growled, and roared and howled" (line 19)? Identify them on the chart below.

Device 1: _____   Device 2: _____

6. **Reading Strategy:** When you **analyze poetic effects,** you identify the way a sound device suggests an image or an emotional response.

   (a) What mood do lines 49-52 create?

_____

   (b) What sound devices contribute to this mood?

_____

Writing

Analysis of a Symbol

A symbol is a sign, word, phrase, image, or other object that stands for or represents something else. For example, a flag can symbolize a country. A fine car can symbolize wealth.

In "The Rime of the Ancient Mariner," the albatross is a poetic symbol—a concrete image that stands for a cluster of ideas. Write an essay analyzing the meanings that the albatross has in the poem.

- Prewrite by gathering details about the albatross. As you work, consider these questions:

1. What does the albatross mean to the sailors when it first appears?

_____

2. How does the mariner act when he recalls shooting the albatross?

_____

3. What are the effects of the bird's death on the crew and on the mariner?

_____

4. Why do you think the albatross finally falls off the mariner's neck and sinks into the sea?

_____

5. At the end of the poem, what lesson does the mariner teach the wedding guest?

_____

6. How is this lesson related to the death of the albatross?

_____

- After listing details, group related details under headings, such as "Luck," "Guilt," and "Respect for Natural Things."

(Heading)	(Heading)	(Heading)	(Heading)
Details:	Details:	Details:	Details:
Details:	Details:	Details:	Details:
Details:	Details:	Details:	Details:

- As you draft your essay on separate paper, use your headings as a guide. Discuss the details under each heading. Link details to your conclusions about the meaning of the albatross.
- Finally, review your draft to highlight flat, unexciting language. Replace such language with vivid, specific words or descriptions.
- Share your analysis with a partner. Ask for feedback on your ideas.

Ode on a Grecian Urn

John Keats

Summary

Keats's poem is addressed to an ancient Grecian urn and contains thoughts about beauty and truth inspired by the urn. The urn is decorated with the following scenes and details: men or gods pursuing young women, a musician, trees, a priest leading a young cow to be sacrificed, and the empty town from which the priest and others have come. Keats reflects that those who are depicted pursuing the women will never catch them. However, they will also never grow old. Although the urn is not subject to suffering and death, it can be "a friend to" humans in their suffering. From its lofty position, the urn seems to say, "Beauty is truth, truth beauty."

Visual Summary

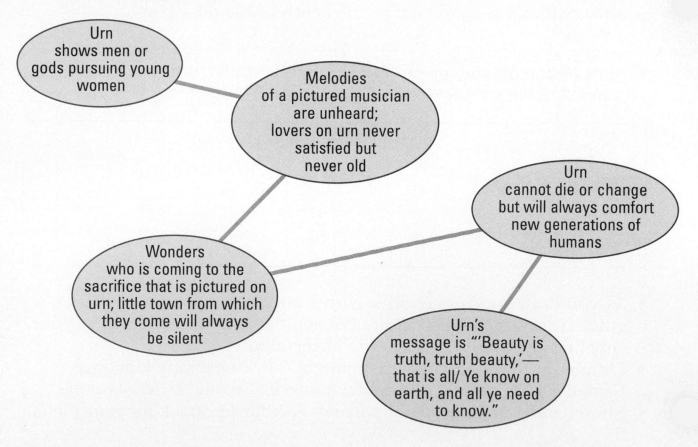

Urn shows men or gods pursuing young women

Melodies of a pictured musician are unheard; lovers on urn never satisfied but never old

Wonders who is coming to the sacrifice that is pictured on urn; little town from which they come will always be silent

Urn cannot die or change but will always comfort new generations of humans

Urn's message is "'Beauty is truth, truth beauty,'— that is all/ Ye know on earth, and all ye need to know."

LITERARY ANALYSIS

The Ode

An **ode** is a lyric poem on a serious subject. Odes usually pay respect to a person or thing. The speaker of the poem addresses that person or thing directly.

John Keats created his own form of the ode. He used ten-line stanzas of iambic pentameter (lines containing ten beats with a repeated pattern of weak-strong beats). Often these stanzas began with a group of four lines rhyming *abab.* The following six lines could be rhymed in various ways. As you read, note the rhyming pattern in Keats's "Ode on a Grecian Urn."

READING STRATEGY

Paraphrasing

Paraphrasing is restating a text in your own words. It can help you understand any difficult work. Use this chart to paraphrase difficult parts of Keats's poem.

Original	Paraphrase
". . . who canst thus express / A flowery tale more sweetly than our rhyme"	Who can tell a beautiful story better than I can tell it in verse?

◆ Vocabulary and Pronunciation

Many words in English have different meanings, depending on their part of speech.

(1) What does *still* mean as an adjective?

_____

(2) What does the same word mean as an adverb?

_____

◆ Stop to Reflect

Personification gives human qualities to something nonhuman. Circle three words or phrases that the speaker uses to personify the urn.

◆ Reading Check

The **setting** is the time and place of an event or a work.

(1) In what region of the world does the scene on the urn take place?

_____

_____

(2) At what period in history does this scene occur?

_____

_____

_____

Ode on a Grecian Urn
John Keats

Thou still unravished[1] bride of quietness
Thou foster child of silence and slow time,
Sylvan[2] historian, who canst thus express
A flowery tale more sweetly than our
   rhyme:
5   What leaf-fringed legend haunts about thy
   shape
Of <u>deities</u> or mortals, or of both,
In Tempe[3] or the <u>dales</u> of Arcady?[4]
What men or gods are these? What
   maidens loath?[5]
What mad pursuit? What struggle to
   escape?
10 What pipes and timbrels?[6] What wild
   <u>ecstasy</u>?

◆ ◆ ◆

On the urn there is a picture of a young man. He seems to be singing of his love for a young woman. Unlike love in the real world, their love will last forever. Another picture on the urn shows a procession and a sacrifice in an ancient little town. The speaker wonders about the occasion for the ceremony. But the urn will not reveal the secret.

◆ ◆ ◆

Vocabulary Development

deities (DEE uh teez) *n.* gods
dales (DAYLZ) *n.* valleys
ecstasy (EK stuh see) *n.* great joy

---

1. **unravished** *adj.* pure.
2. **Sylvan** (SIL vuhn) *adj.* rustic; representing the woods or forest.
3. **Tempe** (TEM pee) valley in Greece that has become a symbol of supreme rural beauty.
4. **Arcady** (AR kud dee) region in Greece that has come to represent the peace and contentment of countryside surroundings.
5. **loath** (LOHTH) *adj.* unwilling.
6. **timbrels** (TIM bruhlz) *n.* tambourines.

O Attic[7] shape! Fair attitude! With brede[8]
Of marble men and maidens overwrought,[9]
With forest branches and the trodden[10]
    weed;
Thou, silent form, dost tease us out of
    thought
15 As doth eternity: Cold Pastoral![11]
When old age shall this generation waste,
Thou shalt remain, in midst of other woe
Than ours, a friend to man, to whom thou
    say'st
"Beauty is truth, truth beauty,"—that is all
20 Ye know on earth, and all ye need to know.

◆ **Reading Strategy**

In a **paraphrase,** you use your own words to restate a passage. Paraphrase the bracketed lines.

_____

_____

_____

_____

_____

_____

◆ **Literary Analysis**

An **ode** honors a person or thing. Why do you think the speaker calls the urn a "friend to man" in the final lines?

_____

_____

_____

---

  7. Attic Attica was the region of Greece in which Athens was located; the art of the region was characterized by grace and simplicity.

  8. brede *n.* interwoven pattern.

  9. overwrought *adj.* adorned with.

10. trodden *v.* trampled.

11. Cold Pastoral unchanging rural scene.

© Pearson Education, Inc.

1. How does the speaker directly address the urn in lines 3-4?

_____

_____

2. Describe the scene pictured on the urn in the first stanza (lines 1-10).

_____

_____

3. In line 15, why is the urn like eternity?

_____

_____

4. What message does the urn give to human beings in line 19?

_____

_____

5. **Literary Analysis:** An ode usually honors its subject and addresses it directly. Does Keats treat the subject of this ode (the urn) seriously? Quote from the poem to support your answer.

_____

_____

6. **Reading Strategy:** In a **paraphrase,** you restate a text in your own words. Paraphrase lines 16-18 of the ode.

_____

_____

Listening and Speaking

An Oral Report

Ancient Greek art, literature, sculpture, and mythology had a deep impact on John Keats. In 1816, Keats saw a group of marble sculptures at the British Museum in London, where they were being exhibited for the first time. He went time after time to see these sculptures, sitting in front of them for hours to admire their beauty.

These sculptures, which are still on view at the British Museum today, are called the Elgin Marbles. This name honors Thomas Bruce, Lord Elgin, who brought the sculptures from Greece to England.

- With a group, use library and/or Internet resources to research the Elgin Marbles and their impact on Keats.
- As you prepare your report, divide the following tasks with your group:
    1. Explain what the Elgin Marbles are and where they came from.
    2. Explain how Keats came to know them
    3. Show the influence of the experience on Keats's poetry
- Make notes on separate paper.
- Then present your findings in an oral report to the class as a whole.

from **A Vindication of the Rights of Woman**

Mary Wollstonecraft

Summary

Writing in the late eighteenth century, Mary Wollstonecraft disapproves of the way in which women are educated. She thinks they are brought up to be attractive rather than to be strong and useful. They are brought up to inspire love rather than respect. It is only through marriage that women can advance in the world. Then, when they marry, they act like children rather than mature adults. The encouragement of weakness in women tends to make them shrewd and domineering, not strong. Despite these general conditions, some women clearly show more sense than their male relatives.

Visual Summary

Causes	Effects
• Women are educated to be attractive rather than strong and useful. • Women can only advance through marriage.	• Women try to inspire love rather than respect. • Women have only a few minor accomplishments. • Women prefer pleasure to ambition. • When women marry, they act like children rather than mature adults. • Women tend to be shrewd and domineering rather than direct and strong.

LITERARY ANALYSIS

Social Commentary

Social commentary is writing or speech that gives insights into society. There are two types of social commentary.

- *Unconscious* social commentary occurs when a writer reflects the social customs of the time without directly discussing them.
- *Conscious* social commentary occurs when a writer directly states that social customs are the cause of a problem.

As you read this selection, analyze the ways in which Mary Wollstonecraft links social customs with the unequal position of women in England during her day.

READING STRATEGY

Determining the Writer's Purpose

When you are reading, try to determine the **writer's purpose**, or what he or she wants to accomplish. Your background knowledge and clues such as the title of the work will help you identify the writer's purpose. Use this chart to help you.

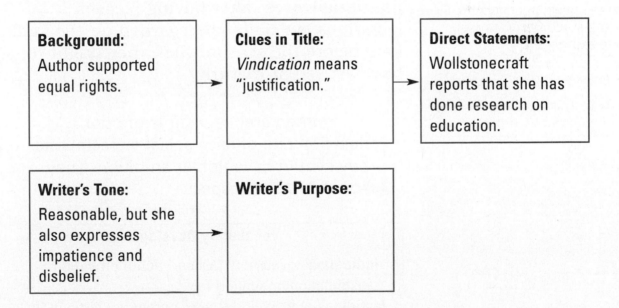

Background:
Author supported equal rights.

Clues in Title:
Vindication means "justification."

Direct Statements:
Wollstonecraft reports that she has done research on education.

Writer's Tone:
Reasonable, but she also expresses impatience and disbelief.

Writer's Purpose:

from A **Vindication** of the Rights of Woman

Mary Wollstonecraft

Wollstonecraft has studied history and the world. She concludes that either people are very different from one another or civilization has been unfair.

◆ ◆ ◆

I have turned over various books written on the subject of education, and patiently observed the conduct of parents and the management of schools; but what has been the result?—a profound conviction that the neglected education of my fellow creatures is the grand source of the misery I deplore, and that women, in particular, are rendered weak and wretched by a variety of concurring[1] causes, originating from one hasty conclusion. The conduct and manners of women, in fact, evidently prove that their minds are not in a healthy state; for, like the flowers which are planted in too rich a soil, strength and usefulness are sacrificed to beauty; and the flaunting leaves, after having pleased a <u>fastidious</u> eye, fade, disregarded on the stalk, long before the season when they ought to have arrived at maturity.

◆ ◆ ◆

Women are the victims of poor education and of false social expectations. They should have nobler ambition. They should demand respect.

◆ ◆ ◆

Vocabulary Development

vindication (vin duh KAY shun) *n.* act of providing justification or support for

fastidious (fa STID ee uhs) *adj.* particular; difficult to please

---

1. **concurring** *adj.* joining together.

◆ **Reading Strategy**

How do the words *misery* and *deplore* give clues to the **author's purpose?**

_____

_____

_____

◆ **Read Fluently**

Read the bracketed passage aloud. What unfortunate fact about the position of women does the author's comparison help to express?

_____

_____

_____

Indeed the word masculine is only a bugbear;[2] there is little reason to fear that women will acquire too much courage or <u>fortitude</u>, for their apparent inferiority with respect to bodily strength must render them in some degree dependent on men in the various relations of life; but why should it be increased by prejudices that give a sex to virtue, and confound[3] simple truths with sensual <u>reveries</u>?

◆ ◆ ◆

Mistaken ideas about women deprive them of a good education and of equality. These ideas also cause some women to act slyly and childishly. Many individual women, however, have more sense than their male relatives and husbands.

Mark the Text

◆ **Literary Analysis**

Besides their dependence on men, what additional problems do women face, according to the author's **social commentary** here? Circle the words that give the answer.

◆ **English Language Development**

If you break down a long sentence, you can often discover the author's main idea. Reread the bracketed sentence word by word. Now write the meaning of the sentence in your own words.

_____

_____

_____

_____

_____

_____

Vocabulary Development

fortitude (FORT uh tood) _n._ courage; strength to endure

reveries (REV uh reez) _n._ daydreams

---

2. bugbear _n._ frightening imaginary creature, especially one that frightens children.

3. confound _v._ confuse by mixing together.

1. What is the author's attitude toward her subject?

_____

_____

2. What emotional words does Wollstonecraft use?

_____

_____

3. What comparison does Wollstonecraft use to describe the current state of women?

_____

_____

4. According to Wollstonecraft, what makes women dependent on men to some degree?

_____

_____

5. **Literary Analysis:** Wollstonecraft writes conscious **social commentary** by singling out a problem in society and identifying the reasons for it. What does she say is the main reason for women's inequality?

_____

_____

6. **Reading Strategy:** What is the **writer's purpose** or goal in this passage? Write two clues you used to determine the purpose.

Writer's Purpose: _____

Clue #1: _____

Clue #2: _____

Writing

Letter to an Author

Write a letter to Mary Wollstonecraft, in which you agree or disagree with her ideas. For example, you might agree with her views about the education of women, while disagreeing with her comments on some women's sly or childish behavior.

As you work, consider the following guidelines:

- Begin by jotting down your reactions to the author's opinions on separate paper. Find specific passages with which you agree or disagree.

- As you draft your letter, keep your audience and purpose in mind. To earn the author's respect, use Standard English and a respectful tone. To catch her interest, choose words that convey enthusiasm for the topic.

- Review your word choice to make sure it sets a tone that fits your purpose and audience. Circle sentences that seem uninteresting or poorly worded. Revise these sentence to create an appropriate, consistent tone.

- Share your letter by reading it aloud to a small group of classmates.

The Lady of Shalott
Alfred, Lord Tennyson

Summary

The Lady of Shalott lives on an island in a river. This river flows down to Camelot, the town where King Arthur has his court. She is a weaver and has heard that she will be cursed if she looks "down to Camelot." She views the world through the mirror hung before her loom, or weaving machine. Often she likes to weave into her cloth the scenes from outdoors that she sees reflected in the mirror. One day she sees in her mirror Sir Lancelot, King  Arthur's greatest knight, as he rides by on the way to Camelot. She is disturbed by the sight, the mirror cracks, and she realizes that the curse is taking effect. She leaves her home, finds a boat, and paints on it *The Lady of Shalott*. Then she gets in the boat and begins drifting toward Camelot. Singing, she dies before the boat reaches the town. The residents of Camelot come out and wonder who the dead woman is. Lancelot says to himself, "She has a lovely face; . . ."

Visual Summary

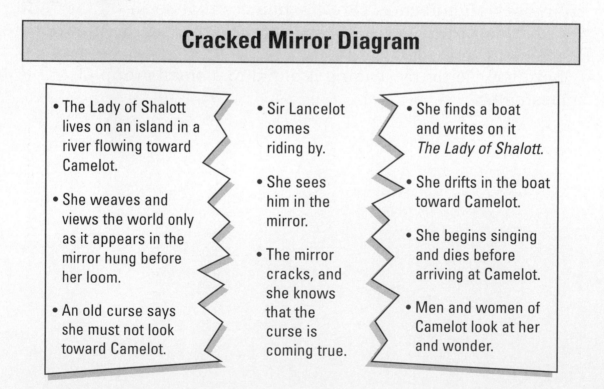

Cracked Mirror Diagram

- The Lady of Shalott lives on an island in a river flowing toward Camelot.

- She weaves and views the world only as it appears in the mirror hung before her loom.

- An old curse says she must not look toward Camelot.

- Sir Lancelot comes riding by.

- She sees him in the mirror.

- The mirror cracks, and she knows that the curse is coming true.

- She finds a boat and writes on it *The Lady of Shalott*.

- She drifts in the boat toward Camelot.

- She begins singing and dies before arriving at Camelot.

- Men and women of Camelot look at her and wonder.

LITERARY ANALYSIS

The Speaker

The **speaker** is the person who says the words of a poem. It isn't necessarily the poet. In a **narrative poem,** or one that tells a story, the speaker is sometimes a character in the story and sometimes a narrator who stands outside the story and tells us what happened. In either case, the speaker provides details about events, characters, and settings as well as his or her feelings about them.

"The Lady of Shalott" is a narrative poem. As you read it, look for the details the speaker provides and his feelings about them. Record the information on this chart.

	Events	Characters	Settings
Details			
Speaker's Feelings			

READING STRATEGY

Judging a Poet's Message

Most poems convey messages about life. When you **judge a poem's message,** you decide how true and useful its message is. First, use the details in the poem to determine the poet's message about life. Next, compare that message to your own experiences in life. Last, make a judgment about whether the poet's message is true and valuable.

Poet's Message	vs.	My Own Experiences	=	**My Judgment**

The Lady of Shalott

Alfred, Lord Tennyson

According to legend, King Arthur ruled England from a place called Camelot (KAM uh lot). There he invited all the great knights of the day. The Shalott (shuh LOT) of this poem is an island in the river that flows to Camelot.

◆ ◆ ◆

On either side the river lie
Long fields of barley and of rye,
That clothe the wold[1] and meet the sky;
And through the field the road runs by
    To many-towered Camelot,
And up and down the people go,
Gazing where the lilies blow
Round an island there below,
    The island of Shalott.

◆ ◆ ◆

The Lady of Shalott lives in a gray-towered castle on the island. No one ever sees her. They do hear her singing. She sits at a loom, a device for weaving yarn into fabric. The loom has a mirror over it.

◆ ◆ ◆

There she weaves by night and day
A magic web with colors gay.
She has heard a whisper say,
A curse is on her if she stay
    To look down to Camelot.
She knows not what the curse may be,
And so she weaveth steadily,
And little other care hath she,
    The Lady of Shalott.

---

1. **wold** *n.* rolling land.

And moving through a mirror clear
That hangs before her all the year,
Shadows of the world appear.
There she sees the highway near
    Winding down to Camelot:

◆ ◆ ◆

    The Lady of Shalott sees all of life, from
weddings to funerals, in her mirror.

◆ ◆ ◆

And sometimes through the mirror blue
The knights come riding two and two:
She hath no loyal knight and true,
    The Lady of Shalott.

◆ ◆ ◆

    The Lady of Shalott grows tired of
looking at a shadow world. One day she sees
the knight Sir Lancelot in her mirror.

◆ ◆ ◆

His broad clear brow in sunlight glowed;
On burnish'd[2] hooves his war horse trode;[3]
From underneath his helmet flowed
His coal-black curls as on he rode,
    As he rode down to Camelot.
From the bank and from the river
He flashed into the crystal mirror,
"Tirra lirra,"[4] by the river
    Sang Sir Lancelot.

She left the web, she left the loom,
She made three <u>paces</u> through the room,
She saw the waterlily bloom,
She saw the helmet and the plume,[5]
    She looked down to Camelot.

Vocabulary Development

paces (PAY suhz) *n.* Steps made walking back and forth

---

2. **burnish'd** *adj.* polished; shining.
3. **trode** *v.* trod; walked.
4. **Tirra lirra** a meaningless sound for singing, like "Tra-la-la."
5. **plume** *n.* the feather on Lancelot's helmet.

© Pearson Education, Inc.

◆ **English Language Development**

Poets often use unusual word order different from that of regular speech. Rewrite the underlined sentence in natural word order.

_____

_____

_____

◆ **Literary Analysis**

What impression does the **speaker** give of Sir Lancelot? Circle the letter of the best answer below.

(a) young and foolish

(b) handsome and cheerful

(c) strange and mysterious

(d) dark and gloomy

Now circle details in the bracketed stanza that help convey this impression.

(1) Why do you think the Lady of Shalott risks the curse and does what's forbidden?

_____

_____

(2) Based on her behavior, what do you think the **poet's message** is?

_____

_____

(3) Do you agree with the message? Why, or why not?

_____

_____

◆ Culture Note

A **superstition** is a belief that is not reasonable. Instead it relies on magic or the idea of good and bad luck. For instance, many cultures have a superstition that breaking a mirror brings bad luck. What other superstitions can you think of?

_____

_____

◆ Read Fluently

Read the five bracketed lines aloud. Try to capture the music.

(1) Give one example of *alliteration,* or repeated consonant sounds at the start of words.

_____

(2) Give one example of *rhyme* at the end of lines.

_____

(3) Give one example of a *repeated word.*

_____

Out flew the web and floated wide;
The mirror cracked from side to side;
"The curse is come upon me," cried
    The Lady of Shalott.

◆ ◆ ◆

    The Lady of Shalott goes down to the river. She finds a boat, unties it, and lies down in it. The river carries the boat downstream.

◆ ◆ ◆

Lying, robed in snowy white
That loosely flew to left and right—
The leaves upon her falling light—
Through the noises of the night
    She floated down to Camelot:
And as the boathead[6] wound along
The willowy hills and fields among,
They heard her singing her last song,
    The Lady of Shalott.

Heard a <u>carol</u>, mournful, holy,
Chanted loudly, chanted <u>lowly</u>,
Till her blood was frozen slowly,
And her eyes were darkened wholly,
    Turned to towered Camelot.
For ere[7] she reached upon the tide
The first house by the waterside,
Singing in her song she died,
    The Lady of Shalott.

◆ ◆ ◆

---

6. **boathead** *n.* the front of the boat.
7. **ere** (AYR) *adv.* before.

As the boat drifts into Camelot, the knights and ladies come to see who is inside. On the prow, or front, of the boat, they read the name, *The Lady of Shalott*.

◆ ◆ ◆

Who is this? and what is here?
And in the lighted palace near
<u>Died the sound of royal cheer</u>;
And they crossed themselves for fear,
    All the knights at Camelot:
But Lancelot <u>mused</u> a little space;[8]
He said, "She has a lovely face;
God in his mercy lend her grace,[9]
    The Lady of Shalott."

◆ **Vocabulary and Pronunciation**

Lowly usually means "of low rank or little importance." What is the meaning here? How do you know?

lowly:

_____

Explanation:

_____

_____

◆ **English Language Development**

As you know, poetry sometimes uses inverted, or switched, word order. Rewrite the underlined clause in natural word order.

_____

_____

Vocabulary Development

mused (MYOOZD) *v.* thought about; considered

---

8. **a little space** some; a bit.
9. **grace** *n.* divine love and protection.

1. What is life on Shalott like for the Lady of Shalott? Circle the letter of the best answer.

   (a) joyous and exciting　　　(c) full of worry about money

   (b) safe but lonely　　　　　(d) dangerous and scary

2. Complete this chain of events to show the main events in the poem.

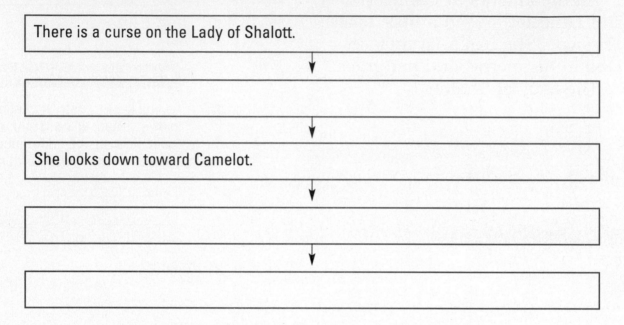

   There is a curse on the Lady of Shalott.

   ↓

   [   ]

   ↓

   She looks down toward Camelot.

   ↓

   [   ]

   ↓

   [   ]

3. (a) What things are brightly colored in the poem?

   _____

   _____

   (b) What things seem to be dull in color?

   _____

   _____

   (c) Explain what the contrast might mean or show about the Lady of Shalott's life.

   _____

   _____

5. **Literary Analysis:** What does the **speaker** seem to think about the Lady of Shalott and her story? For example, does he admire or sympathize with her? Does he think she did the right thing?

_____

_____

6. **Reading Strategy:** Put a check in front of each message that you think the poem conveys. Then choose one, circle it, and **judge** it on the lines below. Say whether you agree or disagree, and give examples from experience to support your opinion.

_____ You need to take chances to be happy in life.

_____ Human beings need other human beings.

_____ No one can live forever on daydreams.

_____ Having a crush on someone always leads to sorrow.

_____ It is not always possible to fulfill our dreams.

_____ The real world is different from what we imagine.

Judgment:

_____

_____

Listening and Speaking

News Report

Imagine that Camelot has TV and that you are a news anchor. Present a news report about the discovery of the Lady of Shalott's body.
- On separate paper, jot down details about the Lady of Shalott's situation in life.
- On your paper, list the events that led to her death.
- Use the details and events you listed in a news report that tells _who, what, where, when, how,_ and _why._
- Rehearse before giving the final report live or on videotape.

My Last Duchess
Robert Browning

Summary

As the poem begins, the Duke is showing a man a painting of the Duke's first wife, who is now dead. The man is an agent representing the father of the woman the Duke hopes to marry. The Duke tells the man that his first wife was "Too easily impressed" by whatever she saw or by whatever anyone did for her. He did not like the way she seemed to rank his "gift" of a great family "name" as equal to "anybody's gift." The Duke did not lower himself to scold her about this. Instead, he "gave commands;/Then all smiles stopped together." The two men begin to leave. The Duke tells the agent that he knows his demands for an adequate dowry, property due to him as the groom, will be met by the new bride's father. At the end, the Duke points out another work of art to the agent.

Visual Summary

Present Tense Within Poem

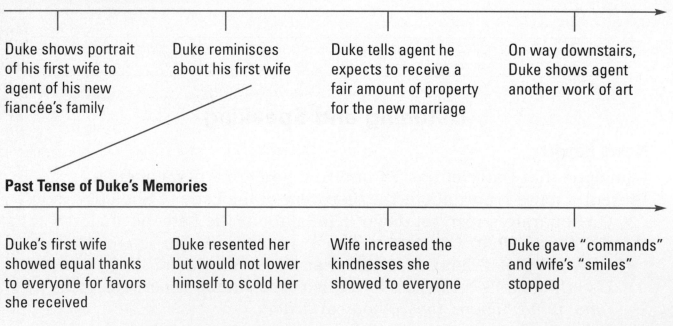

| Duke shows portrait of his first wife to agent of his new fiancée's family | Duke reminisces about his first wife | Duke tells agent he expects to receive a fair amount of property for the new marriage | On way downstairs, Duke shows agent another work of art |

Past Tense of Duke's Memories

| Duke's first wife showed equal thanks to everyone for favors she received | Duke resented her but would not lower himself to scold her | Wife increased the kindnesses she showed to everyone | Duke gave "commands" and wife's "smiles" stopped |

LITERARY ANALYSIS

Dramatic Monologue

A **dramatic monologue** is a long speech by one character. Though dramatic monologues are often parts of plays or other longer works, Robert Browning specialized in short poems that are dramatic monologues all on their own. Browning's dramatic monologues have these elements:

- A speaker whose remarks reveal his or her situation and character.
- A silent listener that the speaker talks to.

Look for these elements as you read "My Last Duchess."

READING STRATEGY

Making Inferences about a Speaker

An **inference** is a reasonable guess that you make from the details you are given. When you read a dramatic monologue, you use the speaker's words and actions to **make inferences** about the speaker's personality, attitudes, and situation.

As you read "My Last Duchess," fill out this chart. Use the speaker's words and actions to make inferences about his character and situation.

Speaker's Words/Actions	Inferences
"That's my last Duchess painted on the wall, / Looking as if she were alive. I call / That piece a wonder . . ."	The Duke seems to care more about owning a fine piece of art than about his wife's death.

My Last Duchess
Robert Browning

The Duke of Ferrara is an Italian nobleman in the 1500s. He has lost his first wife after just three years of marriage. Now he hopes to wed the daughter of another nobleman, a Count. He is speaking to the Count's representative about the planned marriage.

◆ ◆ ◆

That's my last Duchess painted on the wall,
Looking as if she were alive. I call
That piece a wonder, now: Frà Pandolf's[1]
  hands
Worked busily a day, and there she stands.

◆ ◆ ◆

The Duke explains that the joy on the Duchess's face did not only come from her husband's presence.

◆ ◆ ◆

          She had
A heart—how shall I say?—too soon made
  glad,
Too easily impressed; she liked <u>whate'er</u>
She looked on, and her looks went
  everywhere.

◆ ◆ ◆

Everything pleased her—the Duke's love, the setting sun, a small gift, even the mule she rode.

◆ ◆ ◆

◆ **Literary Analysis**

(1) Who is the speaker of this **dramatic monologue?**

_____

(2) Who is the person spoken to?

_____

(3) Explain the situation that brings the two together.

_____

_____

◆ **Vocabulary and Pronunciation**

A *Duchess* (DUCH uhs) is the wife of a *Duke.* What do you think the wife of a *Count* is called?

_____

◆ **English Language Development**

Poets sometimes leave out letters to create a certain rhyme. For example, they say *o'er* instead of *over* in order to have a one-syllable word instead of two. The **apostrophe** (') shows where one or more letters have been left out. Squeeze in the missing letter in the underlined word.

Mark the Text

1. **Frà Pandolf's** work of Brother Pandolf, an imaginary painter.

She thanked men—good! but thanked
Somehow—I know not how—<u>as if she ranked</u>
<u>My gift of a nine-hundred-years-old name</u>
<u>With anybody's gift.</u>

◆ ◆ ◆

Her attitude disgusted the Duke. But he
would not lower himself to correct
something so small. He is a man who never
stoops.

◆ ◆ ◆

Oh sir, she smiled, no doubt,
Whene'er I passed her; but who passed
    without
Much the same smile? This grew; I gave
    commands;
Then all smiles stopped together. There she
    stands
As if alive. Will 't please you rise?

◆ ◆ ◆

As they head downstairs, the Duke
mentions the Count's daughter's fine dowry,
or property she will bring to the marriage. He
also points out a bronze statue of the Roman
sea god Neptune.

◆ ◆ ◆

Notice Neptune, though,
Taming a sea horse, thought a <u>rarity</u>,
Which Claus of Innsbruck[2] cast in bronze for
    me!

◆ **Reading Strategy**

Based on the underlined remark, what **inferences** do you make about the Duke's personality? Circle the word below that best describes him.

modest   proud   democratic

◆ **Reading Strategy**

What **inference** do you make about the Duke from the way he moves on to discuss another piece of art? Answer by completing this sentence:

The Duke cares more about

_____

_____

than he does about

_____

_____

_____ .

Vocabulary Development

rarity (RAYR uh tee) *n.* something unusual and valuable

---

2. **Claus of Innsbruck** an imaginary Austrian sculptor.

1. Put a check in front of all the statements that correctly describe the painting of the Duchess.

   ____ The Duchess is standing.

   ____ The Duchess has a look of deep sorrow on her face.

   ____ The painting is a poorly done work by an artist of little talent.

   ____ The artist is named Claus of Innsbruck.

   ____ The painting is remarkably lifelike.

2. What sort of person was the Duchess? Circle the letter of the answer that best describes her.

   (a) a snob who liked only rich and high-born people

   (b) a kind, warm lady who was easily pleased

   (c) a cold woman not capable of love

   (d) a spoiled brat who flirted with anyone and everyone

3. What sort of marriage do you think the Duke and Duchess had? Circle *happy* or *unhappy*. Then explain your answer on the lines below.

   They probably had a (happy/unhappy) marriage.

   Explanation:

   _____

   _____

   _____

4. **Literary Analysis:** Who are the speaker and listener in this **dramatic monologue**? What situation has brought them together?

   Speaker: _____

   Listener: _____

   Situation: _____

5. **Reading Strategy:** Put a check in front of each **inference** you can make about the Duke's personality, attitudes, and situation. Then list details that lead you to make these inferences.

Possible Inferences	Details
____ He is very proud and snobbish.	
____ He is very affectionate.	
____ He is quite wealthy.	
____ He is very possessive.	

Writing

Recommendation

Should the Count let his daughter marry the Duke? If you were the Count's representative who meets with the Duke, what would you recommend? Give your advice in a written recommendation.

1. List details about the meeting with the Duke.

- Where did you meet?

_____

- What did you see?

_____

- For about how long did you meet?

_____

2. List details from the poem that reveal the Duke's personality or the nature of his first marriage.

_____

_____

3. On separate paper, write your recommendation. Begin with a statement saying whether or not you recommend the marriage. Then use some or all of the details you listed to support your opinion.

from **Hard Times**
Charles Dickens

Summary

Mr. Gradgrind, who runs a school, lectures its students on the importance of facts. He calls on a girl named Sissy Jupe and, learning her name, tells her to change it to Cecilia. On hearing her father works with horses, he asks her to define a horse. She cannot do so. Then, a boy drily defines a horse as "Quadruped. Graminivorous. Forty teeth . . ." and wins Gradgrind's approval. A government officer tells the children not to wallpaper or carpet a room with designs of items that might not themselves really appear on the walls or the floor. He tells them that the only acceptable decorations are "mathematical figures." Finally, a teacher named M'Choakumchild teaches the students in such a way as to discourage the exercise of imagination.

Visual Summary

Purpose Chart	
Purpose	**Details That Support Purpose**
• To humorously criticize the philosophy called utilitarianism (yo͞o til´ə ter´ ē ən iz´ əm), which emphasizes facts and discourages imagination	• Thomas Gradgrind lectures students on the importance of facts. • He wants students to define a horse in a dull, dry way. • A government official wants students to keep to facts by not decorating walls or floors. • A teacher named M'Choakumchild discourages imagination.

LITERARY ANALYSIS

The Novel and Social Criticism

A **novel** is a long work of fiction that has some or all of these features:

- A fairly complicated **plot,** or sequence of events
- Many **settings** in which events occur
- Main **characters** and less important, or **minor,** ones
- One or more **themes** expressing general ideas about life

Though, like all fiction, novels have imaginary characters and events, they also may include some real history as part of their setting. When they do, they may make **social criticism,** calling attention to problems in society.

Hard Times takes place England in the 1800s. As you read this part of the novel, look for the criticisms it makes about English schools of that time and the teaching methods they used.

READING STRATEGY

Recognizing the Writer's Purpose

All forms of writing have a purpose. For example, an author may write to entertain, to convey character's personalities, to describe a scene, to poke fun at human behavior, or to reveal a truth about life. **Recognizing the writer's purpose** can help you understand a novel better. Look for clues about the writer's purpose in the events, characters' conversations, the writer's comments about characters, and other details. Keep track of them on this diagram.

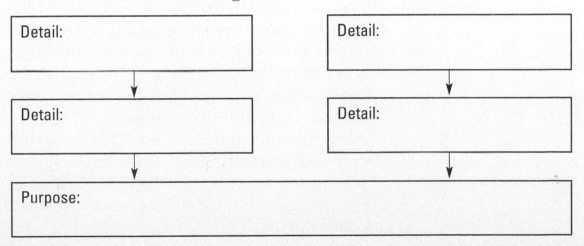

Coke is a coal product used as a fuel in industry or left over when other fuels burn.

What **social criticism** is Dickens making by calling the city Coketown?

_____

_____

Homophones are words with the same sound but different spellings and meanings. A *principle* is a basic rule. A *principal* is the head of a school; it can also mean "main" or "most important."

In the underlined sentence, circle three words that have homophones. Write them and their homophones below. Then write the meanings of each word and its homophone below.

(1) Word _____

Meaning _____

Homophone _____

Meaning _____

(2) Word _____

Meaning _____

Homophone _____

Meaning _____

(3) Word _____

Meaning _____

Homophone _____

Meaning _____

from **Hard Times**
Charles Dickens

In the industrial city of Coketown, England, a rich retired businessman named Gradgrind has started a school for poor children. Gradgrind believes that facts and logic must rule all activities. He feels that everything can be weighed and measured and that material things will make people happy. He explains his ideas when he meets with a government official and the teacher he has hired, Mr. M'Choakumchild.

◆ ◆ ◆

"Now, what I want is, Facts. Teach these boys and girls nothing but Facts. Facts alone are wanted in life. Plant nothing else, and root out everything else. You can only form the minds of reasoning animals upon Facts: nothing else will ever be of any service to them. This is the <u>principle</u> on which I bring up my own children, and this is the principle on which I bring up these children. Stick to Facts, sir!"

<u>The scene was a plain, bare, monotonous vault of a schoolroom.</u>

◆ ◆ ◆

The children are seated in number order. Mr. Gradgrind thinks of them as little pitchers, waiting to have facts poured into them. Now he addresses the class.

◆ ◆ ◆

"Girl number twenty," said Mr. Gradgrind, squarely pointing with his square forefinger, "I don't know that girl. Who is that girl?"

"Sissy Jupe, sir," explained number twenty, blushing, standing up, and curtseying.

"Sissy is not a name," said Mr. Gradgrind. "Don't call yourself Sissy. Call yourself Cecilia."

"It's father as calls me Sissy, sir," returned the young girl in a trembling voice, and with another curtsey.

"Then he has no business to do it," said Mr. Gradgrind. "Tell him he mustn't. Cecilia Jupe. Let me see. What is your father?"

"He belongs to the horse-riding, if you please, sir."

◆ ◆ ◆

Sissy's father rides horses in the circus. Mr. Gradgrind does not approve of this job. He tells Sissy to say that her father trains and shoes horses and treats them when they are ill. He continues:

◆ ◆ ◆

"Give me your definition of a horse."
(Sissy Jupe thrown into the greatest alarm by this demand.)

"Girl number twenty unable to define a horse!" said Mr. Gradgrind, for the general behoof[1] of all the little pitchers. "Girl number twenty possessed of no facts, in reference to one of the commonest of animals! Some boy's definition of a horse. Bitzer, yours."

◆ ◆ ◆

Bitzer is the sort of "pitcher" Mr. Gradgrind likes. He has an excellent memory and has absorbed many facts. He is a pale, freckled boy with cold eyes.

◆ ◆ ◆

"Quadruped.[2] Graminivorous.[3] Forty teeth, namely twenty-four grinders, four eye-teeth, and twelve incisive. Sheds coat in the spring; in marshy countries, sheds hoofs, too. Hoofs hard, but requiring to be shod with iron.[4] Age known by marks in mouth." Thus (and much more) Bitzer.

"Now girl number twenty," said Mr. Gradgrind. "You know what a horse is."

◆ ◆ ◆

---

1. **behoof** (bi HUF) *n.* behalf; benefit.
2. **Quadruped** (KAWD ruh ped) *n.* an animal with four legs.
3. **Graminivorous** (gram uh NIV uh ruhs) *adj.* grass-eating.
4. **shod with iron** shoed with iron horseshoes to protect the horses' feet.

from Hard Times **133**

◆ **English Language Development**

The description of Sissy's reaction in parentheses is actually not a complete sentence. It's missing part of the verb. Squeeze in a word that would make the description a complete sentence.

◆ **Read Fluently**

Read aloud Mr. Gradgrind's words in the underlined passage. Try to use the tone of voice he might have used. How do you think Sissy felt when she heard these words?

_____

_____

_____

◆ **Reading Strategy**

Put a check in front of each choice that might be the **writer's purpose** in this bracketed passage. Check at least two.

____ to introduce the character of Bitzer to readers

____ to poke fun at the facts-only method of teaching

____ to help readers understand what a horse is

____ to poke fun at Mr. Gradgrind

Children is the plural of *child:*

1 *child*   2 or more *children*

Most English words form their plurals by adding *s* or *es.* But a few, like *child,* are irregular. Write the irregular plural form of each word listed below. Then say all the words aloud.

(1) 1 foot, 2 or more

_____

(2) 1 gentleman, 2 or more

_____

(3) 1 mouse, 2 or more

_____

(4) 1 woman, 2 or more

_____

What is Sissy's reason for wanting a carpet with pictures of flowers?

_____

_____

_____

_____

The other visitor now steps forward. He is a government official who has spent his life following petty rules and dull routine.

◆　◆　◆

"Now, let me ask you girls and boys. Would you paper a room with <u>representations</u> of a horse?"

After a pause, one half of the children cried in chorus, "Yes, sir!" Upon which the other half, seeing in the gentleman's face that Yes was wrong, cried out in chorus, "No, sir!"—as the custom is, in these examinations.

"Of course, No. Why wouldn't you?"

◆　◆　◆

The children have no idea. The visitor points out that horses never walk up and down rooms in reality. So it makes no sense to have them do it on wallpaper. Then he asks if the students would get a carpet with pictures of flowers on it. By now, most of the children know they should answer "No." A few still say "Yes," including Sissy Jupe.

◆　◆　◆

Sissy blushed, and stood up.

"So you would carpet your room—or your husband's room, if you were a grown woman, and had a husband—with representations of flowers, would you," said the gentleman. "Why would you?"

"If you please, sir, I am very fond of flowers," returned the girl.

"And is that why you would put tables and chairs upon them, and have people walking over them with heavy boots?"

Vocabulary Development

representations (rep ruh zen TAY shuhnz) *n.* pictures; illustrations

---

"It wouldn't hurt them, sir. They wouldn't crush and <u>wither</u> if you please, sir. They would be the pictures of what was very pretty and pleasant, and I would fancy—"

"Ay, ay, ay! but you mustn't fancy," cried the gentleman, quite <u>elated</u> by coming so happily to his point. "That's it! You are never to fancy."

"You are not, Cecilia Jupe," Thomas Gradgrind solemnly repeated, "to do anything of that kind."

"Fact, fact, fact!" said the gentleman. And "Fact, fact, fact!" repeated Thomas Gradgrind.

◆ ◆ ◆

The official tells Sissy to forget the word *fancy,* for it is the very opposite of *fact.* Then he asks Mr. M'Choakumchild to begin teaching the first lesson.

◆ ◆ ◆

So, Mr. M'Choakumchild began in his best manner. He and some one hundred and forty other schoolmasters, had been lately turned at the same time, in the same factory, on the same principles, like so many pianoforte[5] legs.

◆ ◆ ◆

Mr. M'Choakumchild has learned the facts in a long list of subjects. He knows all about language, geography, and science.

◆ ◆ ◆

<u>If he had only learnt a little less, how infinitely better he might have taught much more!</u>

Vocabulary Development

wither (WITH uhr) *v.* shrivel up; dry out, wrinkle, and die
elated (i LAY tid) *adj.* excited

---

5. **pianoforte** (PYAN oh fawrt) *n.* an old term for a piano.

◆ **Literary Analysis**

The *M'* in the teacher's name is an old way of writing *Mc.*

(1) What does the rest of the teacher's name suggest? Explain below.

Choakumchild:

_____

_____

(2) What **social criticism** is Dickens making about Mr. M'Choakumchild and the way he was taught to teach?

_____

_____

◆ **Reading Check**

Explain what the underlined statement means by completing the sentence below.

If Mr. M'Choakumchild only

_____

he would be

_____

_____

1. Circle two words below that best describe Mr. Gradgrind.

   rich   romantic   kind

   opinionated   clever   shy

2. Why does Mr. Gradgrind have a say in the way the children at the school are taught?

   _____

3. *Grind* can mean "to work or study very hard" or "a boring routine." Explain these characters' names and why they are appropriate.

   • Gradgrind:

   _____

   • M'Choakumchild:

   _____

4. **Literary Analysis:** On the lines, list two problems in the schools that Dickens points out in his **social criticism** in this part of the novel.

   • _____

   _____

   • _____

   _____

5. **Reading Strategy:** Based on this selection, check two items below that most seem to be the **writer's purpose** in writing *Hard Times.*

   ____ to entertain by poking fun at some teaching methods of the day

   ____ to create a detailed character sketch of Sissy Jupe

   ____ to draw attention to problems at schools like the one described

   ____ to stress the importance of facts and fact checking

Listening and Speaking

Debate

Working in small teams, hold a debate about a basic value or teaching method in education today. For example, two teams might debate the value of computers in the classroom or the value of standardized tests to assess students' yearly progress.

1. Choose the subject for your debate.

_____

_____

_____

2. Do some research at the library or on the Internet to help you decide on the main points you want to make.

3. Jot down the main points, along with some supporting details.

_____

_____

_____

4. Practice making those points in debate rehearsals with others on your team.

5. Hold the actual debate in front of the rest of the class.

from Jane Eyre
Charlotte Brontë

Summary

In this chapter of the novel, Jane is at a boarding school for orphan girls called Lowood. She describes the harsh physical conditions, the lack of sufficient food for the girls, and the cruel way in which one of the teachers, Miss Scatcherd, treats a girl named Helen Burns. Later, Jane has the opportunity to speak with Helen in private. Jane is surprised by Helen's acceptance of the wrongs done to her.

Visual Summary

Comparison and Contrast of Characters		
	Jane Eyre	**Helen Burns**
Similarities	• student at Lowood, a school for orphan girls • thoughtful and intelligent	• student at Lowood, a school for orphan girls • thoughtful and intelligent
Differences	• new student • one of the younger girls • says she would not patiently accept unjust treatment	• not a new student • one of the older girls • accepts the unjust treatment she receives and blames herself

LITERARY ANALYSIS
The Novel and Social Criticism

A **novel** is a long work of fiction. Like all fiction, novels tell of imaginary people and events. A novel usually has these features:

- A fairly complicated **plot**, or sequence of events
- Many **settings**, or times and places, in which events occur
- Main **characters** and less important, or minor, ones
- One or more **themes** expressing general ideas about life

Even though they are fiction, novels sometimes include real history or current events as part of their settings. When they do, they may include **social criticism** calling attention to problems in society. *Jane Eyre*, for example, takes place in early nineteenth-century England. As you read this section of the novel, look for the criticisms it makes about English schools of that time.

READING STRATEGY
Recognizing the Writer's Purpose

All forms of writing have a purpose. For example, an author may write to entertain, to poke fun at human behavior, or to reveal a truth about life. **Recognizing the writer's purpose** can help you understand a novel better. Look for clues about the writer's purpose in the following:

- The events
- The characters' conversations
- The writer's comments about characters
- Other details

from Jane Eyre

Charlotte Brontë

After Jane Eyre's parents die, her selfish aunt sends her to a school for poor girls called Lowood. The school is a grim place with a strict routine that Jane does not like. Little money is spent on the girls' food or comfort. Though it is January, there is almost no heat. Jane, who is telling the story, has been at Lowood for two days.

◆ ◆ ◆

The next day <u>commenced</u> as before, getting up and dressing by rushlight;[1] but this morning we were <u>obliged</u> to <u>dispense</u> with the ceremony of washing: the water in the pitchers was frozen. . . . Before the long hour and a half of prayers and Bible reading was over, I felt ready to <u>perish</u> with cold. Breakfast time came at last. . . . How small my portion seemed! I wished it had been double.

◆ ◆ ◆

Jane is unfamiliar with the school routine. She is glad when her lessons end at three o'clock and she is given a hem to sew. But some older girls are still reading with Miss Scatcherd, the history teacher. The girls are seated with the best reader first. The best reader is a girl who spoke kindly to Jane the day before. Jane is surprised when the teacher suddenly sends this girl from first to last place for no very good reason.

◆ ◆ ◆

Vocabulary Development

commenced (kuh MENST) *v.* began
obliged (uh BLĪJD) *v.* forced
dispense (dis PENS) *v.* give up
perish (PER ish) *v.* die

---

1. **rushlight** cheap, smelly, smoky lighting obtained from burning rushes, or reeds, twisted together and dipped in wax.

Miss Scatcherd continued to make her an object of constant notice: she was continually <u>addressing</u> to her such phrases as the following:—

"Burns" (such it seems was her name: the girls here, were all called by their <u>surnames</u>,[2] as boys are elsewhere), "Burns, you are standing on the side of your shoe, turn your toes out immediately." "Burns, you poke your chin most unpleasantly, draw it in." "Burns, I insist on your holding your head up: I will not have you before me in that attitude," etc. etc.

A chapter having been read through twice, the books were closed and the girls examined. . . . every little difficulty was solved instantly when it reached Burns: her memory seemed to have retained the substance of the whole lesson, and she was ready with answers on every point. I kept expecting that Miss Scatcherd would praise her attention; but, instead of that, she suddenly cried out:—

"You dirty, disagreeable girl! you have never cleaned your <u>nails</u> this morning!"

Burns made no answer: I wondered at her silence.

"Why," thought I, "does she not explain that she could neither clean her nails nor wash her face, as the water was frozen?"

♦ ♦ ♦

Jane is called away by another teacher. That teacher needs help winding thread for sewing. When Jane returns to her seat, Miss Scatcherd has just sent Burns to get a bundle of twigs used as a punishment rod.

♦ ♦ ♦

Vocabulary Development

addressing (uh DRES ing) *v.* talking to

2. **surnames** (SUR naymz) last names; family names.

from Jane Eyre **141**

◆ **Culture Note**

A surname is a family name, which in English comes last. For example, in *Jane Eyre, Eyre* is Jane's family name. In many Asian cultures, however, the family name comes first. What is the style used in your native land? To answer, write your name as it is written in your native land, and circle the family name:

_____

◆ **Reading Strategy**

Circle the letter of the choice that states the **writer's purpose** here. Then, on the lines below, explain how you know this is the purpose.

The writer wants to show

(a) an English history lesson.

(b) Jane's dislike for school.

(c) the importance of good manners.

(d) the unfair treatment of Burns.

_____

_____

_____

◆ **Reading Check**

Who seems to be Miss Scatcherd's brightest student? Write your answer here:

_____

Then circle the details that tell you.

The suffix *-ly* is sometimes added to adjectives to turn them to adverbs of manner. For example,

quiet + *ly* = *quietly*,

which means "in a quiet, or soft-spoken, manner." Circle two more adverbs of manner in this sentence. Then, on the lines below, explain their meanings.

(1) _____

_____

(2) _____

_____

◆ **Reading Strategy**

What can you learn about Jane from her conversation with Burns? Circle the correct answer.

(a) She is unfriendly.

(b) She is curious and friendly.

(c) She is rude and impolite.

(d) She hopes Burns will be her best friend.

. . . then she <u>quietly</u>, and without being told, unloosed her pinafore,[3] and the teacher instantly and sharply inflicted on her neck a dozen strokes with the bunch of twigs. Not a tear rose to Burns's eye; and, while I paused from my sewing, because my fingers quivered at this spectacle with a sentiment of unavailing and impotent anger, not a feature of her <u>pensive</u> face altered its ordinary expression.

"Hardened girl!" exclaimed Miss Scatcherd, "nothing can correct you of your <u>slatternly</u> habits: carry the rod away."

Burns obeyed: I looked at her narrowly as she emerged from the book closet; she was just putting back her handkerchief into her pocket, and the trace of a tear glistened on her thin cheek.

◆ ◆ ◆

Soon it is evening play hour. This time is Jane's favorite time at school so far. Still hungry, she is glad to have a bit of bread and coffee. She then looks for Burns and finds her reading by the fireplace.

◆ ◆ ◆

I sat down by her on the floor.
"What is your name besides Burns?"
"Helen."
"Do you come a long way from here?"
"I come from a place further north; quite on the borders of Scotland."
"Will you ever go back?"
"I hope so; but nobody can be sure of the future."

Vocabulary Development

pensive (PEN siv) *adj.* serious; thoughtful
slatternly (SLAT ern lee) *adj.* like a slob; very sloppy

---

3. **pinafore** (PIN uh for) *n.* an overdress of light fabric resembling an apron and bib.

"You must wish to leave Lowood?"

"No: why should I? I was sent to Lowood to get an education; and it would be of no use going away until I have attained that object."

"But that teacher, Miss Scatcherd, is so cruel to you?"

"Cruel? Not at all! She is severe: she dislikes my faults."

"And if I were in your place I should dislike her: I should resist her; if she struck me with that rod, I should get it from her hand; I should break it under her nose."

"Probably you would do nothing of the sort: but if you did, Mr. Brocklehurst[4] would expel you from the school; that would be a great grief to your relations. It is far better to endure patiently a smart[5] which nobody feels but yourself, than to commit a hasty action whose evil consequences will extend to all connected with you—and, besides, the Bible bids us return good for evil."

◆ ◆ ◆

Jane does not really understand Helen's views. She feels it makes no sense to reward mean people with kindness and good behavior, for then they will never change. Yet she deeply admires Helen for holding such noble views.

◆ ◆ ◆

"You say you have faults, Helen: what are they? To me you seem very good."

"Then learn from me, not to judge by appearances: I am, as Miss Scatcherd said, slatternly; I seldom put, and never keep, things in order; I am careless; I forget rules; I read when I should learn my lessons; I have no method; and sometimes I say, like you, I cannot bear to be subjected to systematic

4. **Mr. Brocklehurst** the man who runs the school.
5. **smart** pain; sting.

◆ **Literary Analysis**

Put a check in front of any **social criticism** you think this passage helps make.

____ Poor girls often put up with bad treatment to get an education.

____ Family pressure forced the girls to compete to see who was smart.

____ The girls were not treated with the religious ideals they were taught.

____ The schools were so crowded that girls were expelled for no reason.

◆ **Reading Check**

Number the seven faults that Helen says she has.

(1) Why do you think the monitor is mean to Helen?

She is mean because _____

_____

(2) What **social criticism** about schools does her behavior show?

Her behavior shows that in schools _____

_____

arrangements. This is all very <u>provoking</u> to Miss Scatcherd, who is naturally neat, punctual, and particular."

"And <u>cross</u> and cruel," I added; but Helen Burns would not admit my addition: she kept silence. . . .

She was not allowed much time for <u>meditation</u>: a monitor, a great rough girl, presently came up, exclaiming in a strong Cumberland[6] accent—

"Helen Burns, if you don't go and put your drawer in order, and fold up your work this minute, I'll tell Miss Scatcherd to come and look at it!"

Vocabulary Development

provoking (pruh VOH king) *adj.* irritating
cross (KRAWS) *adj.* easily irritated; angry
meditation (med i TAY shun) *n.* deep thought

---

6. **Cumberland** (KUM ber lind) a county in northern England.

1. What sort of school is Lowood? Circle the letter of the best answer.

   (a) a boarding school for wealthy girls

   (b) a charity school for poor girls

   (c) a reform school for girls with criminal records

   (d) an arts school for gifted musicians, painters, and writers

2. Why can't the girls wash up that morning?

   _____

   _____

3. What do Jane and Helen have in common? How are they different? List two similarities and two differences on the chart below.

	Jane	Helen
Similarities		
Differences		

4. Circle the words that best describe Miss Scatcherd.

   strict   fair   mean   bullying   inspiring   timid   disorganized

5. **Literary Analysis:** List four problems in schools like Jane's that the author points out in her **social criticism** in this part of the novel.

   1. _____

   2. _____

   3. _____

   4. _____

from Jane Eyre **145**

6. **Reading Strategy:** Based on this selection, check two items that most seem like the **writer's purpose** in writing *Jane Eyre*.

____ to tell an interesting story about growing up

____ to poke fun at girls' ideas and conversations

____ to draw attention to problems at schools like Lowood

____ to persuade people to send their daughters to schools like Lowood

Writing

Compare and Contrast

Write a paragraph comparing and contrasting Victorian education, as shown in this selection, with your experience of American schools today.

- On the chart below, list similarities and differences. Examples of one similarity and one difference have been done for you.

Jane's School	Today's Schools
Many classes end at 3 PM.	Many classes end at 3 PM.
They study English history.	We study American and world history.

- Complete this general statement about similarities and differences.

Schools today are often more _____ but less _____ than they were in Victorian times.

- On separate paper, use your general statement to open a paragraph comparing and contrasting the schools. Support your opening sentence with some of the similarities and differences you listed.
- Share your paragraph with your classmates.

Journey of the Magi
T. S. Eliot

Summary

In this poem, the speaker is one of the three Magi (mā´ jī´), or wise men, who traveled to Bethlehem to honor the baby Jesus. Now he is an old man, and he reflects on the meaning of the journey he made many years ago. He tells about the various difficulties that he and his companions encountered. Finally, he confesses that the birth he witnessed was like a death, because it was "Hard and bitter" for him and his companions. Having seen the baby Jesus, they returned to their own kingdoms. However, they no longer felt at ease among people who worshiped many gods rather than one.

Visual Summary

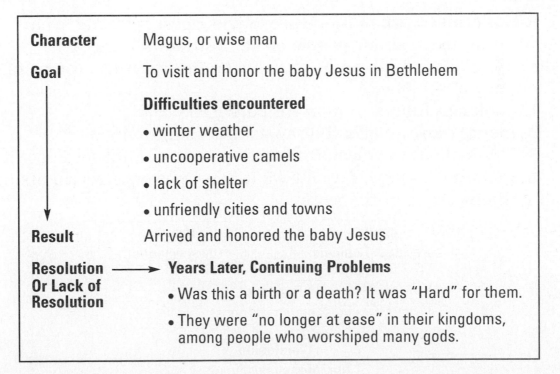

Character	Magus, or wise man
Goal	To visit and honor the baby Jesus in Bethlehem
	Difficulties encountered
	• winter weather
	• uncooperative camels
	• lack of shelter
	• unfriendly cities and towns
Result	Arrived and honored the baby Jesus
Resolution Or Lack of Resolution →	**Years Later, Continuing Problems**
	• Was this a birth or a death? It was "Hard" for them.
	• They were "no longer at ease" in their kingdoms, among people who worshiped many gods.

LITERARY ANALYSIS

Modernism

Modernism was a trend in the arts that took place in the early twentieth century, from about 1890 to 1945. A Modernist work of literature often has the following features:

- It emphasizes **images**, or words and phrases that appeal to one or more of the five senses.
- It relies on the use of the **symbol**—an image, character, object, or action that stands for something beyond itself.
- It contains **allusions**, or indirect references to people, places, events, or works of literature.
- It has few direct statements of thoughts and feelings.
- It does not provide realistic pictures of life.
- It focuses on the spiritual troubles of modern life.

Notice the Modernist elements in the poem "Journey of the Magi."

READING STRATEGY

Interpreting

A Modernist work of literature may suggest a theme, or a central message about people or life, without stating it directly. Follow these steps to help you **interpret** the theme of "Journey of the Magi."

1. Look carefully at important passages.
2. Identify key images that appear more than once.
3. Think about the ideas that these patterns of images suggest.
4. Draw a conclusion about what these patterns reveal about the meaning of the work.

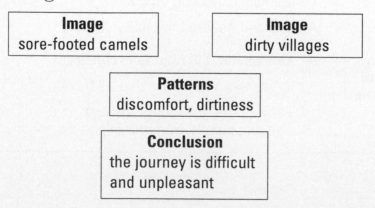

| **Image**
sore-footed camels | **Image**
dirty villages |

Patterns
discomfort, dirtiness

Conclusion
the journey is difficult and unpleasant

Journey of the Magi

T. S. Eliot

"A cold coming we[1] had of it,
Just the worst time of the year
For a journey, and such a long journey:
The ways deep and the weather sharp,
The very dead of winter."[2]

◆　◆　◆

The travelers have difficulty with the camels. They are stubborn and sore and don't want to move.

The speaker says the travelers miss the warm weather and the serving girls at home. Instead they meet cursing camel drivers, have trouble finding shelter, and visit unfriendly and expensive towns.

The travelers finally decide to travel at night. They have little sleep and begin to wonder if their journey is wise.

◆　◆　◆

1. The speaker is one of the three wise men, or magi, who traveled to Bethlehem to visit the baby Jesus. In this poem, the speaker reflects upon the meaning of the journey.
2. "A . . . winter": Adapted from a part of a sermon delivered by 17th-century Bishop Lancelot Andrews: "A cold coming they had of it at this time of year, just the worst time of the year to take a journey, and specially a long journey in. The ways deep, the weather sharp, the days short, the sun farthest off . . . the very dead of winter."

◆ Reading Check

Read the bracketed part of the poem. Circle two difficulties the wise men encountered on their journey.

◆ Vocabulary and Pronunciation

In English, the word *dead* has several different meanings. For example, it can mean "no longer living," "very tired," "no longer in use," "the time of greatest intensity," or "dull." Which meaning of *dead* does Eliot use in the poem?

_____

◆ English Language Development

In English, most adjectives come before the nouns they describe. For example, the adjective *long* comes before the noun *journey* in this line from the poem:

". . . and such a long journey."

In this poem, Eliot often reverses the usual placement of adjectives. List two examples from the poem in which Eliot places the adjective after the noun it describes.

1. _____

2. _____

Circle two images in the bracketed passage that might help you **interpret the theme** of hope and new life.

Which characteristic of **Modernist** poetry does Eliot use in this poem? Circle the letter of the correct answer.

(a) symbol   (b) image

(c) allusion   (d) all of these

Is the speaker's journey positive or negative? Why do you think so?

_____

_____

_____

Then at dawn we came down to a <u>temperate</u>
  valley,
Wet, below the snow line,[3] smelling of
  <u>vegetation</u>;
With a running stream and a water-mill
  beating the darkness,
And three trees[4] on the low sky,

◆ ◆ ◆

The travelers arrive at a tavern but can get no information. They continue and find the place they are looking for that evening.

The speaker says that this journey took place a long time ago. He's not sure whether he witnessed a birth or a death. The miraculous birth of Jesus caused the death of his old world, his old life, and his old beliefs.

Vocabulary Development

temperate (TEM per it) *adj.*   neither hot nor cold
vegetation (vej i TAY shun) *n.*   the plants of an area or
  region

---

3. **snow line** the boundary where a snow-covered area begins.
4. **three trees** a Biblical allusion to the three crosses of Calvary, the hill outside ancient Jerusalem where Jesus and two other men were crucified.

1. What event has the speaker gone to witness?

   _____

   _____

2. At what time of year does the speaker travel?

   _____

   _____

3. What two details help you picture the journey described by the speaker?

   1. _____

   2. _____

4. How does the speaker feel about the event he witnesses?

   _____

   _____

5. **Reading Strategy:** Reread the first stanza. What three images would you use to **interpret the theme**?

   1. _____

   2. _____

   3. _____

6. **Literary Analysis:** What features of **Modernism** does Eliot use in this poem? List three examples on the following chart.

Image	Symbol	Allusion

Writing

Response to Criticism

Read the following comment by Rena Braun: "T.S. Eliot's poem 'Journey of the Magi' describes the journey of the 'Wise men from the East' towards Christ and thus, symbolically, towards Christianity. Many critics parallel the Magi's journey with Eliot's own journey in search of 'satisfaction' in Christianity." Then respond to this comment.

1. What connection does Braun see between the magi's physical journey and Eliot's spiritual journey?

_____

_____

2. Do you agree or disagree with the critic's ideas? Explain why you feel this way.

_____

_____

3. Write one detail from the poem that supports your opinion.

_____

_____

4. Write another detail from the poem that supports your opinion.

_____

_____

5. Write a third detail from the poem that supports your opinion.

_____

_____

On a separate sheet of paper, write a paragraph in which you respond to Rena Braun's statements about "Journey of the Magi."

Shooting an Elephant
George Orwell

Summary

Orwell was a British police officer in Burma, which was then a British colony. He secretly felt that the British should leave Burma. However, he was also very angry at the Burmese who insulted and taunted him. One day, he heard that an elephant had gone wild. Orwell sent for an elephant gun. Then, with the gun, he went looking for the beast, followed by a large crowd. He saw that the elephant was peaceful and sensed that its spell of wildness must have worn off. However, he also knew that he would have to kill it, if only to avoid looking like a fool in front of the Burmese. At that point, he realized that colonizers are not really free in a colonized country: They must always appear to be in control. Finally, he shot the elephant, but it took a long time to die.

Visual Summary

General Situation	Orwell hated colonialism, but he also hated the Burmese who taunted him.
Sequence of Events	Elephant went wild
	Elephant killed laborer
	Orwell got elephant gun and hunted for elephant, trailed by crowd of Burmese
	Orwell shot and killed elephant
Insight	Orwell realized that he would shoot the elephant only because he did not want to look like a fool.
Generalization	Colonizers are not really free, because they must always pretend that they are in control.

LITERARY ANALYSIS

Irony

In literature, **irony** involves the difference, or the contrast, between appearance and reality. Writers may use different types of irony for humorous effect or to drive home an important point. The chart below shows two types of irony:

Types of Irony	
Verbal Irony	the contrast between what a character says and what a character means
Irony of Situation	the contrast between what is expected to happen and what actually does happen

In "Shooting an Elephant," Orwell uses irony to help the reader understand the no-win situation he faced in Burma. In this passage from the essay, Orwell creates irony of situation as he describes how Buddhist priests behave in an unexpected manner.

> The young Buddhist priests were the worst of all. There were several thousands of them in the town and none of them seemed to have anything to do except stand on street corners and jeer at Europeans.

READING STRATEGY

Recognizing the Writer's Attitudes

When you read a work of nonfiction, pay attention to how the writer feels about the topic. **Recognizing the writer's attitudes** can help you evaluate the information the writer provides about a particular subject.

As you read "Shooting an Elephant," follow these steps to identify Orwell's attitudes about British imperialism, about the Burmese, and about the elephant.

1. Read carefully, noting the writer's choice of words and details.
2. Look for important statements about the topic.
3. Draw conclusions about the writer's thoughts or feelings toward the subject.

Shooting an Elephant
George Orwell

The author, George Orwell, is a police officer in Burma. He is hated in this anti-European area. The feelings aren't strong enough for crowds to create a riot, but he is a single target.

◆ ◆ ◆

When a <u>nimble</u> Burman tripped me up on the football field and the referee (another Burman) looked the other way, the crowd yelled with hideous laughter. This happened more than once. In the end the sneering yellow faces of young men that met me everywhere, the insults hooted after me when I was at a safe distance, got badly on my nerves. The young Buddhist priests were the worst of all. There were several thousands of them in the town and none of them seemed to have anything to do except stand on street corners and jeer at Europeans.

◆ ◆ ◆

Orwell is confused and upset by the behavior of the Burmese. He decides that the reason for the problem is imperialism, or the fact that Burma is a colony of Great Britain. Orwell confesses that he sides with the

◆ **Background Note**

In this essay, Orwell writes of the days of English rule in Burma. Burma is a country located in southeast Asia on the Bay of Bengal. Great Britain fought several wars against Burma during the 1800s. The British hoped to gain a better trade route with China. In 1885, Britain finally conquered Burma. Although the British failed to achieve the desired "golden path" to China, Burma provided Britain with other economic opportunities. For example, the British sold Burmese rice to other countries. Many Burmese, however, were unwilling to accept British rule. Opponents of the British formed the People's Volunteer Association, led by Aung San (owng sahn). This group helped win Burma's independence from Britain in 1948.

◆ **Reading Strategy**

Underline two words or phrases that help you recognize **the writer's attitudes** toward the Burmese.

◆ **Reading Check**

How do the Burmese view the English? Give examples to support your answer.

_____

_____

_____

Vocabulary Development

nimble (NIM buhl) *adj.* quick or light in movement

♦ ♦ ♦

One day something happened which in a roundabout way was <u>enlightening</u>. It was a tiny incident in itself, but it gave me a better glimpse than I had had before of the real nature of <u>imperialism</u>—the real motives for which <u>despotic</u> governments act.

♦ ♦ ♦

One morning a <u>subinspector</u> calls Orwell. A loose elephant is destroying the market. The man asks Orwell to do something about the problem.

♦ ♦ ♦

I did not know what I could do, but I wanted to see what was happening and I got onto a pony and started out. I took my rifle, an old .44 Winchester and much too small to kill an elephant, but I thought the noise might be useful . . . .

♦ ♦ ♦

Orwell learns that the elephant is tame. But the elephant is in a temporary, dangerous state of frenzy known as "must." The elephant had escaped from its chains, destroyed a bamboo hut, killed a cow, eaten fruit at some fruit stands, and knocked over a

---

In English, many words beginning with *sub* mean *lower than* something. For example, the word *subdivisional* at the beginning of this essay refers to a unit of government that is *lower than* a division. What does the word *subinspector,* underlined in blue, mean?

_____

_____

_____

What problem does the subinspector call Orwell about?

_____

_____

_____

_____

Vocabulary Development

enlightening (en LĪT en ing) *adj.* giving insight or understanding to

imperialism (im PEE ree uh lizm) *n.* policy of forming an empire and securing economic power by conquest and colonization

despotic (de SPOT ik) *adj.* harsh, cruel, unjust

garbage truck. Orwell joins Burmese and Indian police officers who question residents of a poor neighborhood to find out where the elephant has gone. The men hear a woman yelling at a group of children. Orwell investigates and finds the body of a dead Indian laborer lying in the mud. The man had been killed by the elephant. After finding the man's body, Orwell sends for his elephant rifle. Some Burmese tell Orwell that the elephant is in nearby rice fields. They are excited by the idea that he is going to shoot the elephant. A crowd gathers and follows him. Orwell spots the elephant eating grass by the side of the road.

◆ ◆ ◆

I had halted on the road. As soon as I saw the elephant I knew with perfect certainty that I ought not to shoot him. It is a serious matter to shoot a working elephant—it is comparable to destroying a huge and costly piece of machinery—and obviously one ought not to do it if it can possibly be avoided.

◆ ◆ ◆

At that moment, the elephant seems harmless. Orwell feels that the elephant's frenzy is over and it won't be dangerous. Orwell really doesn't want to shoot him. He decides to watch the elephant for a while before he goes home.

◆ ◆ ◆

But at that moment I glanced round at the crowd that had followed me. It was an immense crowd, two thousand at the least and growing every minute. It blocked the road for a

© Pearson Education, Inc.

◆ **Literary Analysis**

Which type of **irony** does Orwell use in the sentence underlined in blue? Circle the letter of the correct answer.

(a) situational (b) verbal

◆ **Reading Check**

Does Orwell think the elephant is dangerous? Why, or why not?

_____

_____

_____

_____

_____

_____

_____

long distance on either side. I looked at the sea of yellow faces above the <u>garish</u> clothes—faces all happy and excited over this bit of fun, all certain that the elephant was going to be shot. They were watching me as they would watch a conjurer[1] about to perform a trick. They did not like me, but with the magical rifle in my hands I was momentarily worth watching. And suddenly I realized that I should have to shoot the elephant after all. The people expected it of me and I had got to do it; I could feel their two thousand wills pressing me forward, irresistibly. . . .

◆ ◆ ◆

Despite his position of authority, Orwell senses that he must do what the people expect him to do. He does not wish to harm the elephant, especially because the creature is worth more alive. However, he feels he has no choice. He thinks about what might happen if something goes wrong. He believes that the crowd would run him down and trample him to death if he fails to kill the animal. Orwell prepares to shoot the elephant.

◆ ◆ ◆

<u>The crowd grew very still, and a deep, low, happy sigh, as of people who see the theater curtain go up at last, breathed from innumerable throats. They were going to have their bit of fun, after all.</u>

◆ ◆ ◆

Orwell really doesn't know how to shoot an elephant. He should have aimed at the ear hole. Instead, he aims in front of the ear hole, thinking that is where the brain is.

◆ Literary Analysis

What type of **irony**—verbal or situational—lies in Orwell's comments underlined in blue?

_____

_____

_____

Vocabulary Development

garish (GAR ish) *adj.* loud and flashy
innumerable (i NYOO muhr uh bul) *adj.* too many to be counted

---

1. **conjurer** (KAHN juhr uhr) *n.* a magician.

When I pulled the trigger I did not hear the bang or feel the kick—one never does when a shot goes home—but I heard the devilish roar of glee that went up from the crowd.

❖ ❖ ❖

The elephant changes immediately. He doesn't fall at first, but finally he slobbers and sags to his knees. He seems to deteriorate.

❖ ❖ ❖

One could have imagined him thousands of years old. I fired again into the same spot. At the second shot he did not collapse but climbed with desperate slowness to his feet and stood weakly upright, with legs sagging and head drooping. I fired a third time. That was the shot that did for him. You could see the agony of it jolt his whole body and knock the last <u>remnant</u> of strength from his legs.

❖ ❖ ❖

The elephant appears to rise. His trunk reaches skyward as he trumpets, but his hind legs collapse.

❖ ❖ ❖

And then down he came, his belly toward me,

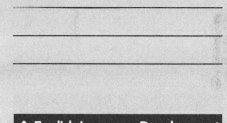

Vocabulary Development

remnant (REM nuhnt) *n.* what is left over

---

with a crash that seemed to shake the ground even where I lay.

◆ ◆ ◆

The elephant is clearly dying, but he is not yet dead. Orwell fires more shots, but the elephant still breathes.

◆ ◆ ◆

In the end I could not stand it any longer and went away. I heard later that it took him half an hour to die. Burmans were bringing dahs[2] and baskets even before I left, and I was told they had stripped his body almost to the bones by the afternoon.

Afterward, of course, there were endless discussions about the shooting of the elephant. The owner was furious, but he was only an Indian and could do nothing.

◆ ◆ ◆

In Burma, the law says that a mad elephant must be killed. Orwell feels that he did the right thing. The Europeans do not agree.

◆ ◆ ◆

And afterward I was very glad that the coolie had been killed; it put me legally in the right and it gave me a sufficient <u>pretext</u> for shooting the elephant. I often wondered whether any of the others grasped that I had done it solely to avoid looking a fool.

Vocabulary Development

pretext (PREE tekst) *n.* excuse

---

2. **dahs** (daz) *n.* knives.

1. How did the Burmese feel about George Orwell?

_____

2. Why did they feel this way?

_____

_____

3. What decision did Orwell make about the elephant, and why did he make this decision?

_____

_____

4. Do you agree with Orwell's decision about the elephant? Why, or why not?

_____

_____

5. **Reading Strategy:** What three words would you use to identify **Orwell's attitudes** toward imperialism?

   1. _____

   2. _____

   3. _____

6. **Literary Analysis:** On the following chart, list two examples of **irony** Orwell uses in this essay.

	Example
Verbal Irony	
Irony of Situation	

Listening and Speaking

Audiovisual Presentation

In this essay, Orwell writes about Burma when it was under British rule. Today, Burma is known as Myanmar (myahn MAH). With a group, use library books, social studies textbooks, magazines, and the Internet to find out about present-day Myanmar. Here are some questions to get you started:

- Where is Myanmar located?

_____

_____

- What form of government exists there today?

_____

_____

- What are some traditional foods?

_____

_____

- What is Myanmar's main religion?

_____

_____

- What are the country's major industries?

_____

_____

- What different kinds of arts are found in Myanmar?

_____

_____

Then, as a group, prepare and deliver an **audiovisual presentation** about Myanmar. Have each group member direct one section of the presentation. Give a brief oral report to share your findings. Use a timeline of important events, a map, charts, photographs, and recordings of Burmese music to bring your presentation to life.

No Witchcraft for Sale
Doris Lessing

Summary

The Farquars are a white couple who own a farm in southern Africa. Their African cook, Gideon, is very fond of their young son, Teddy. However, as Teddy grows older, Gideon senses that the cultural divide between whites and blacks is gradually ending his intimacy with the boy. One day, a snake spits poison into Teddy's eyes. Gideon saves Teddy's sight with medicine from the root of a plant. The Farquars are extremely grateful to Gideon, giving him gifts and raising his pay. When the word of what has happened gets to town, a scientist comes calling on the Farquars. The scientist does not really believe that Gideon has a remedy, but he makes it his business to investigate all stories of cures with medicinal plants. Gideon surprises the Farquars by his resentful and sulky response to the scientist. He takes the Farquars and the doctor on a long walk, finally giving the scientist a common flower that is not the one he used for the cure. Afterward, the Farquars and Teddy tease Gideon about his stubbornness.

Visual Summary

Problems:	• Cultural divide between whites and blacks • Danger that Teddy may lose his vision due to a snake's poison
Events:	1. Poisonous snake spits into Teddy's eyes 2. Gideon finds a root that cures Teddy 3. Farquars reward Gideon 4. Scientist investigates the "cure" 5. Gideon reacts angrily, giving scientist the wrong plant
Resolution:	• Cultural divide between whites and blacks remains, despite mutual affection in some cases

LITERARY ANALYSIS
Cultural Conflict

Many British stories of the mid-twentieth century reflect the conflicts of British colonialism, or the rule of other regions by Britain. These conflicts include political, personal, and cultural conflicts. **Cultural conflicts** are disagreements caused by differences in customs, beliefs, and values.

One cultural conflict in "No Witchcraft for Sale" is caused by differences in the social position held by whites and blacks in Southern Rhodesia. In this passage, for example, a young white boy named Teddy behaves unfairly toward the son of the cook who works for his family:

> Gideon's youngest son, who was now a herdsboy, came especially up from the compound to see the scooter. He was afraid to come near it, but Teddy showed off in front of him. . . . And he raced in circles around the black child until he was frightened, and fled back to the bush.
>
> "Why did you frighten him?" asked Gideon, gravely reproachful.
>
> Teddy said defiantly: "He's only a black boy," and laughed.

READING STRATEGY
Analyzing Cultural Differences

Some stories involve conflicts between cultures. You can **analyze cultural differences** to understand why such conflicts take place. To identify cultural differences, think about the contrast in the values, customs, and beliefs that contribute to the problems between two characters or two groups of characters.

As you read "No Witchcraft for Sale," use this diagram to help you analyze cultural conflict in the story. First, jot down obvious cultural differences between the Farquars and their cook, Gideon. Then tell what customs, beliefs, and values the Farquars and Gideon share.

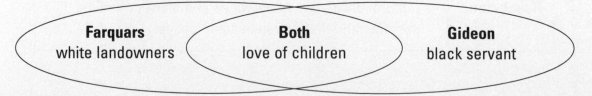

Farquars
white landowners

Both
love of children

Gideon
black servant

No Witchcraft for Sale
Doris Lessing

The Farquars, a white couple in southern Africa, finally have their first child. Their servants bring gifts and love the baby's blonde hair and blue eyes.

◆　◆　◆

They congratulated Mrs. Farquar as if she had achieved a very great thing, and she felt that she had—her smile for the lingering, admiring natives was warm and grateful.

◆　◆　◆

Gideon, the Farquars' cook, affectionately nicknames Teddy "Little Yellow Head." Gideon plays with the little boy and helps him learn how to walk. Mrs. Farquar recognizes Gideon's love for her son and rewards him with a raise in pay. Gideon and Mrs. Farquar notice what happens when a native child and Teddy meet. The children curiously stare at each other's skin, eye, and hair color.

◆　◆　◆

Gideon, who was watching, shook his head wonderingly, and said: "Ah, missus, these are both children, and one will grow up to be a baas,[1] and one will be a servant"; and Mrs. Farquar smiled and said sadly, "Yes, Gideon, I was thinking the same."

◆　◆　◆

Gideon knows that this is God's will. He and the Farquars share the common bond of being very religious.

◆　◆　◆

◆ Culture Note

This story takes place in Southern Rhodesia in southern Africa. Today, the country is called Zimbabwe (zihm BAHB way). By 1924, the year Lessing's family moved there, Rhodesia had been under British control for just over thirty years. Before that, the region had been ruled by a succession of black African empires. Under British and then white Rhodesian rule, the political rights of black Rhodesians were limited. Most blacks were forced to work as low-paid servants. Look at a library book, a social studies textbook, or the Internet to find out more about the political and social history of Zimbabwe.

• Why did Cecil Rhodes bring the British South Africa Company to Rhodesia?

_____

• When did Rhodesia declare its independence from Britain?

_____

• When did blacks in Rhodesia gain equal rights?

_____

• When did Rhodesia officially change its name to Zimbabwe?

_____

---

1. **baas** (bahs) *n.* boss.

◆ **Stop to Reflect**

Teddy and Gideon's son are the same age. But their futures will be very different. What is the difference?

_____

_____

_____

Teddy was about six years old when he was given a scooter, and discovered the <u>intoxications</u> of speed.

◆ ◆ ◆

Teddy races around the farm and into the kitchen. He scares the farm animals and family pets. Gideon laughs as he watches all this activity.

◆ ◆ ◆

Gideon's youngest son, who was now a herdsboy, came especially up from the compound to see the scooter. He was afraid to come near it, but Teddy showed off in front of him. "Piccanin,"[2] shouted Teddy, "get out of my way!" And he raced in circles around the black child until he was frightened, and fled back to the bush.

◆ ◆ ◆

Gideon blames Teddy for frightening his son. Teddy rudely replies that Gideon's son is only a black boy.

Gideon's feelings toward Teddy change. He realizes that Teddy will soon grow up and go away to school. Gideon treats Teddy kindly but acts much less friendly. Teddy, in turn, begins to treat Gideon more like a servant.

◆ ◆ ◆

But on the day that Teddy came staggering into the kitchen with his fists to his eyes, shrieking with pain, Gideon dropped the pot full of hot soup that he was holding, rushed to

◆ **Reading Check**

How does Teddy get hurt?

_____

_____

_____

Vocabulary Development

intoxications (in TAHKS i CAY shunz) *n.* great excitement

---

2. **piccanin** (PIK uh nin) *n.* an offensive term for a native child.

the child, and forced aside his fingers. "A snake!" he exclaimed.

◆ ◆ ◆

As Teddy rested on his scooter, a tree-snake spat right into his eyes. Mrs. Farquar sees that Teddy's eyes are already swollen. She is terrified that Teddy will go blind.

◆ ◆ ◆

Gideon said: "Wait a minute, missus, I'll get some medicine." He ran off into the bush.

Mrs. Farquar lifted the child into the house and bathed his eyes with permanganate.[3] She had scarcely heard Gideon's words; but when she saw that her <u>remedies</u> had no effect at all, and remembered how she had seen natives with no sight in their eyes, because of the spitting of a snake, she began to look for the return of her cook, remembering what she heard of the <u>efficacy</u> of native herbs.

◆ ◆ ◆

Terrified, she holds her son and waits for Gideon to return. Shortly, he appears with a plant. He shows her the root and assures her that it will provide a cure for Teddy's eyes.

◆ ◆ ◆

Without even washing it, he put the root in his mouth, chewed it <u>vigorously</u>, and then held the spittle there while he took the child forcibly

◆ Reading Strategy

Mrs. Farquar and Gideon react differently to Teddy's injury. Underline two words, phrases, or sentences in the bracketed passage that reveal their **cultural differences**.

◆ Reading Check

What does Mrs. Farquar remember about natives she's seen that really frightens her?

_____

_____

_____

Vocabulary Development

remedies (REM i deez) *n.* medicines or therapies that take away pain or cure diseases

efficacy (EF i kuh see) *n.* power to produce intended effects

vigorously (VIG uhr uhs lee) *adv.* forcefully; energetically

---

3. **permanganate** (per MANG guh nayt) *n.* salt of permanganic acid used as a remedy for snake poison.

What is the cause of the **cultural conflict** in this passage? Circle the letter of the correct answer.

(a) Teddy's feelings of superiority

(b) Gideon's knowledge of native medicine

(c) Mrs. Farquar's religious beliefs

(1) What is the result of Gideon's medicine?

_____

_____

(2) What do the Farquars do to reward Gideon?

_____

_____

_____

_____

from Mrs. Farquar. He gripped Teddy down between his knees, and pressed the balls of his thumbs into the swollen eyes, so that the child screamed and Mrs. Farquar cried out in protest: "Gideon, Gideon!"

◆　◆　◆

Gideon ignores her and opens Teddy's eyes to spit into them. When he is finished, he promises Mrs. Farquar that Teddy will be fine. But she finds this hard to believe.

◆　◆　◆

In a couple of hours the swellings were gone: the eyes were <u>inflamed</u> and tender but Teddy could see. Mr. and Mrs. Farquar went to Gideon in the kitchen and thanked him over and over again.

◆　◆　◆

They do not know how to express their gratitude. They give Gideon gifts and a raise, but nothing can really pay for Teddy's cured eyes.

◆　◆　◆

Mrs. Farquar said: "Gideon, God chose you as an instrument for His goodness," and Gideon said: "Yes, missus, God is very good."

◆　◆　◆

The story of how Gideon saved Teddy's eyesight spreads throughout the area. The whites are frustrated because they do not know what plant Gideon used. The natives will not tell them. A doctor in town hears the story but does not really believe it.

Vocabulary Development

inflamed (in FLAYMD) *adj.* reddened

One day a scientist from the nearby laboratory arrives. He brings a lot of equipment.

◆   ◆   ◆

Mr. and Mrs. Farquar were flustered and pleased and flattered. They asked the scientist to lunch, and they told the story all over again, for the hundredth time. Little Teddy was there too, his blue eyes sparkling with health, to prove the truth of it.

◆   ◆   ◆

The scientist explains that people everywhere would benefit if the drug that helped Teddy could be available to them. The Farquars are pleased at the idea of being able to help.

◆   ◆   ◆

But when the scientist began talking of the money that might result, their manner showed discomfort.

◆   ◆   ◆

They do not want to think of money in connection with the miracle that has happened. The scientist realizes that they feel this way and reminds them that they can help others.

After eating their meal, the Farquars tell Gideon why the scientist came to visit. Gideon seems surprised and angry. Mr. Farquar tells Gideon that thousands of people could be cured by the medicine he used to save Teddy. Gideon listens but stubbornly refuses to reveal what root he used. The Farquars realize Gideon will not tell them what they want to know. To Gideon, the Africans' traditional knowledge of plant medicine, which is passed on from generation to generation, represents power and wisdom. Suddenly, however, Gideon agrees to show the root to the Farquars and the scientist. On an extremely hot afternoon,

---

◆ **Read Fluently**

Read the bracketed paragraphs aloud. What three words or phrases suggest the Farquars' mixed feelings about the scientist's visit?

1. _____

2. _____

3. _____

◆ **Vocabulary and Pronunciation**

In English, most words beginning with *dis* mean *not* something. For example, the word *discomfort* in this paragraph means *lack of comfort*. What does the word *distasteful* mean?

_____

_____

_____

◆ **Reading Check**

How does Gideon respond when he hears the reason for the scientist's visit?

_____

_____

_____

_____

the group silently walks for two hours. Gideon appears to search for the root.

◆ ◆ ◆

At last, six miles from the house, Gideon suddenly decided they had had enough; or perhaps his anger <u>evaporated</u> at that moment.

◆ ◆ ◆

Gideon finally picks up flowers just like ones they have seen all along their journey. He hands them to the scientist and leaves the group to go home.

When the scientist stops in the kitchen to thank Gideon, he is gone. He's back to prepare dinner, but it is days before he and the Farquars are friends again.

◆ ◆ ◆

The Farquars made inquiries about the root from their laborers. Sometimes they were answered with distrustful stares. Sometimes the natives said: "We do not know. We have never heard of the root."

◆ ◆ ◆

A cattle boy who has worked for the family for a long time tells them to ask Gideon. He says that Gideon is the son of a famous medicine man and can cure anything, although he is not as good as a white doctor.

◆ ◆ ◆

After some time, when the soreness had gone from between the Farquars and Gideon, they began to joke: "When are you going to show us the snake-root, Gideon?" And he would laugh

Vocabulary Development

evaporated (ee VAP uh ray tid) *v.* disappeared

© Pearson Education, Inc.

and shake his head, saying, a little uncomfortably: "But I did show you, missus, have you forgotten?"

◆ ◆ ◆

Later, even Teddy teases Gideon about tricking everyone about the cure for the snake bite.

◆ ◆ ◆

And Gideon would <u>double up</u> with polite laughter. After much laughing, he would suddenly straighten himself up, wipe his old eyes, and look sadly at Teddy, who was grinning <u>mischievously</u> at him across the kitchen: "Ah, Little Yellow Head, how you have grown! Soon you will be grown up with a farm of your own. . . ."

Vocabulary Development

mischievously (MIS chuh vuhs lee) *adv.* playfully

1. What happens to Teddy's eyes?

_____

_____

2. How does Gideon save Teddy's sight?

_____

_____

3. Why does Gideon refuse to share his knowledge with the Farquars and the scientist?

_____

_____

4. Do you agree with Gideon's decision to keep information about the plant to himself? Why, or why not?

_____

_____

5. **Reading Strategy: Analyze cultural differences** in this story. List one value or belief the Farquars and Gideon share and one value or belief that sets them apart.

   1. _____

   2. _____

6. **Literary Analysis:** On the following chart, list one incident that reflects **cultural conflict** between whites and blacks in the story.

Farquars' Values	Incident	Gideon's Values

Writing

Problem-and-Solution Essay

In this story, the Farquars and Gideon have a problem. The Farquars cannot understand why Gideon will not tell them what he knows about the snake root. Gideon feels betrayed by the Farquars. Prepare to write a **problem-and-solution essay.** Identify the problem and offer a few possible solutions to the problem.

- State the problem in your own words.

_____

_____

- Propose one possible solution.

_____

_____

- Explain each of the steps that should be taken to put this solution into action.

_____

_____

- Propose another possible solution.

_____

_____

- Explain each of the steps that should be taken to put this solution into action.

_____

_____

- Propose a third possible solution.

_____

_____

- Explain each of the steps that should be taken to put this solution into action.

_____

_____

Araby
James Joyce

Summary

The narrator tells about an experience he had as a boy growing up in Dublin, Ireland, in the late nineteenth century. He had a crush on another boy's sister. The first time she spoke to him, she asked whether he was going to a fair called *Araby*. She herself could not go. However, he offered to bring her something from *Araby*. He asked his uncle—he lived with his uncle and aunt— for the money to go to the fair. The night of the fair, his uncle came home late, and it was after nine when he gave the narrator the money. By the time the narrator arrived at the fair, it was nearly over. The big hall in which the fair was being held was already dark. At one stall, a young woman with an English accent was talking and laughing with two young men. The narrator refused her offer to serve him. He suddenly realized that he had been foolish about everything, and he felt both grief and anger.

Visual Summary

Exposition	Rising Action	Climax	Falling Action	Resolution
• narrator was a young boy in Dublin • had a crush on another boy's sister	• he offered to bring her a gift from *Araby* • uncle came back late the night of the fair, and it was after nine when narrator got the money to go	• narrator got to fair late	• big hall was already darkened • at one stall, narrator saw young woman • she asked him if he wanted anything, and he said no	• in a sudden flash, narrator realized how foolish he had been about everything • felt grief and anger

LITERARY ANALYSIS

Plot Devices

A **plot device** is a particular technique used to build a story. Writers often use plot devices to achieve a special effect. One kind of plot device developed by James Joyce is an **epiphany** (ee PIF uh nee).

- An **epiphany** is a character's sudden insight.
- It reveals an important truth.
- It occurs during an ordinary event or situation.
- It forms the climax, or the high point of interest or suspense, of the story.

In "Araby," the events in the story lead up to the narrator's epiphany:

> Gazing up into the darkness <u>I saw myself as a creature driven</u> . . . <u>by vanity</u>; and my eyes burned with anguish and anger.

READING STRATEGY

Picturing the Action and Situation

When you read a story, use your imagination to help you **picture the action and situation**. This strategy may help you understand the characters, the setting, or the events in a story.

1. Briefly stop when you come to a difficult passage.
2. Pay attention to details.
3. Try to picture the scene in your mind.
   - What is happening?
   - Where are these events taking place?
   - How do the characters react to these events?
4. Use a graphic organizer like the one shown to put what you "see" into words.

Story Passage	Action and Situation
Then I turned away slowly and walked down the middle of the bazaar. I allowed the two pennies to fall against the sixpence in my pocket.	The narrator is shopping in the bazaar. He feels overwhelmed, discouraged, and confused. He has not yet bought anything.

◆ **Background Note**

This story takes place in Dublin, Ireland, in the early 1900s. The main character is a boy who lives on North Richmond Street and goes to a bazaar. Like the narrator in "Araby," James Joyce, the story's author, once lived with his family on North Richmond Street. When Joyce was twelve years old, he went to the Araby bazaar held in Dublin in May 1894. Look at a library book, a social studies textbook, or the Internet to find a map of Dublin. Use the map to answer the following questions:

• What river flows through the city?

_____

• What is the name of one park in Dublin?

_____

• In what part of Dublin does the narrator live with his aunt and uncle?

_____

◆ **Reading Strategy**

Circle words and phrases in the bracketed paragraph here and on page 177 that help you form a mental **picture** of the scene.

Araby
James Joyce

The narrator, or storyteller, lives on a quiet, dead-end street. He enjoys playing on the street with his friends. They explore the dark alleys, gardens, and stables behind the houses. In the winter, the boys stay out until dark. From the shadows they watch the narrator's uncle come home. They also watch the sister of a boy whose last name is Mangan. The narrator has a serious crush on Mangan's sister. Every morning he watches her door until she comes out. Then he follows her when she goes to school. He even thinks about her when he helps his aunt with her shopping in the busy, dirty markets in Dublin. Although the narrator has strong feelings for Mangan's sister, he has never said a single word to her.

◆ ◆ ◆

At last she spoke to me. When she <u>addressed</u> the first words to me I was so confused that I did not know what to answer. She asked me was I going to *Araby*. I forget whether I answered yes or no. It would be a splendid bazaar,[1] she said; she would love to go.

"And why can't you?" I asked.

While she spoke she turned a silver bracelet round and round her wrist. She could not go, she said, because there would be a retreat[2]

Vocabulary Development

addressed (uh DREST) *v.* directed to

---

1. **bazaar** (buh ZAHR) *n.* a market or fair where various goods are sold in stalls.
2. **retreat** (ri TREET) *n.* period of retirement or seclusion for prayer, religious study, and meditation.

that week in her convent.[3] Her brother and two other boys were fighting for their caps and I was alone at the railings. She held one of the spikes, bowing her head towards me. The light from the lamp opposite our door caught the white curve of her neck, lit up her hair that rested there and, falling, lit up the hand upon the railing. It fell over one side of her dress and caught the white border of a petticoat,[4] just visible as she stood at ease.

◆ ◆ ◆

Mangan's sister is happy for the narrator. He promises to bring her something from the bazaar.

The narrator cannot stop thinking about Mangan's sister. He is excited about going to the bazaar. He has trouble doing his schoolwork, and he daydreams in class. On Saturday morning the narrator reminds his uncle that he wants to go to the bazaar that night. His uncle leaves for the day. While the narrator eagerly waits for his uncle to return and give him money, he stares at the clock. He stands at the window for an hour and watches his friends play outside. He pictures Mangan's sister in his mind.

◆ ◆ ◆

At nine o'clock I heard my uncle's latchkey in the hall door. I heard him talking to himself and heard the hallstand rocking when it had received the weight of his overcoat. I could interpret these signs. When he was midway through his dinner I asked him to give me the money to go to the bazaar. He had forgotten.

"The people are in bed and after their first sleep now," he said.

3. **convent** (KAHN vent) *n.* school run by an order of nuns.
4. **petticoat** (PET ee koht) *n.* a woman's slip that is sometimes full and trimmed with lace or ruffles.

© Pearson Education, Inc.

Araby **177**

◆ **Read Fluently**

Read the first bracketed paragraph out loud. Before you read, skim through the paragraph to look for words you do not know. Make sure you know what they mean and how to pronounce them, so that you can read smoothly.

◆ **Reading Check**

Why does the narrator have to wait to go to the bazaar?

_____

_____

_____

◆ **Reading Strategy**

In this paragraph, the narrator hears his uncle coming in. Circle the details that tell him what his uncle is doing.

Mark the Text!

Read the bracketed paragraph aloud. Write three words you would use to describe the narrator's uncle.

1. _____

2. _____

3. _____

I did not smile. My aunt said to him energetically:

"Can't you give him the money and let him go? You've kept him late enough as it is."

My uncle said he was very sorry he had forgotten. He said he believed in the old saying: *All work and no play makes Jack a dull boy.* He asked me where I was going and, when I had told him a second time he asked me did I know *The Arab's Farewell to His Steed.*[5] When I left the kitchen he was about to recite the opening lines of the piece to my aunt.

◆　◆　◆

The narrator leaves the house with money his uncle gives him. He rides an empty train to the bazaar. The train arrives just before ten o'clock. The narrator pays the fee and enters a large, dark hall. Because it is late, most of the stalls are closed. The bazaar is as quiet as a church.

◆　◆　◆

The word *stall* has several different meanings. For example, it can mean "a sudden loss of power in an engine," "a booth at a market," or "a section for an animal in a barn." Which meaning of *stall* does Joyce use here?

_____

_____

Remembering with difficulty why I had come I went over to one of the <u>stalls</u> and examined porcelain[6] vases and flowered tea sets. At the door of the stall a young lady was talking and laughing with two young gentlemen. I <u>remarked</u> their English accents and listened vaguely to their conversation.

"O, I never said such a thing!"

"O, but you did!"

"O, but I didn't!"

"Didn't she say that?"

"Yes. I heard her."

"O, there's a . . . fib!"

Vocabulary Development

remarked (ri MARKT) *v.* noticed

---

5. **The Arab's. . .His Steed** *n.* popular nineteenth-century poem.
6. **porcelain** (POR suh lin) *n.* a hard, white type of clay pottery also known as china.

The young lady offers to help the narrator. He answers that he doesn't need help, and she doesn't encourage him. She watches him as she returns to the conversation with the two young gentlemen.

The narrator lingers and pretends to be interested in the items in the stall. Then, he leaves, jingling the coins in his pocket.

♦ ♦ ♦

I heard a voice call from one end of the gallery that the light was out. The upper part of the hall was now completely dark.

Gazing up into the darkness I saw myself as a creature driven and <u>derided</u> by <u>vanity</u>; and my eyes burned with anguish and anger.

◆ **Reading Check**

Why doesn't the young lady spend more time helping the narrator at her stall?

◆ **Stop to Reflect**

Is the narrator's trip to Araby a success? Why, or why not?

_____

_____

_____

◆ **Literary Analysis**

The last paragraph is the narrator's **epiphany**. Tell in your own words what the narrator realizes about himself in the **epiphany**.

_____

_____

_____

◆ **English Language Development**

In English, many adverbs are formed by adding -*ly* to an adjective. For example, the word *slowly* is an adverb. It is formed by adding -*ly* to the adjective *slow*. What is another adverb that appears in the bracketed paragraph?

_____

Vocabulary Development

derided (dee RĪD id) *v.* made fun of

vanity (VAN uh tee) *n.* excessive pride

---

1. How does the narrator feel about Mangan's sister?

_____

2. Where does the narrator want to go?

_____

3. Why does he want to go there?

_____

4. Why does the narrator fail to achieve his goal? Name three reasons.

1. _____

2. _____

3. _____

5. **Reading Strategy:** Choose a scene in "Araby." Then **picture the action and situation** in your mind. Complete this chart to tell which scene you pictured and what you learned about the characters in the story.

Situation	Character's Actions	Character's Feelings

6. **Literary Analysis:** James Joyce uses the **plot device** of an **epiphany** in "Araby." List two words or phrases in the story that reveal the narrator's feelings about himself after the epiphany.

1. _____

2. _____

Writing

Personal Essay

A **personal essay** expresses your views on a certain topic. Get ready to write a personal essay about the epiphany, or the moment of sudden insight, that the narrator has at the end of "Araby."

- What do you think the narrator learns about himself at the end of the story?

  _____

  _____

- Write one quotation from the story that supports your ideas.

  _____

  _____

- Do you agree with the narrator's opinion of himself? Tell why or why not.

  _____

  _____

- Write one quotation from the story that supports your ideas.

  _____

  _____

- Is the narrator's experience positive or negative? Tell what you think and why.

  _____

  _____

- Write one quotation from the story that supports your ideas.

  _____

  _____

Now number your notes in the order you would present them in a personal essay about the epiphany in Joyce's story. Write 1 next to the idea you would present first, 2 next to the idea you would present second, and so on.

Reading Informational Materials

Part 2 contains the **Reading Informational Materials** features from *Prentice Hall Literature: Timeless Voices, Timeless Themes* with reading support and practice.

- Review the **Reading Informational Materials** page. You will use the information and skills on this page as you read the selection.

- Read the selection, and respond to the questions. Look for the **Mark the Text** logo for special help with interactive reading.

- Use the **Reading Informational Materials** questions at the end of each selection to build your understanding of various types of informational materials.

- Use the **Review and Assess** questions at the end of each selection to review what you have read and to check your understanding.

About Maps

The purpose of a **map** is to present geographical information in a convenient graphic form. To use a map effectively, you should be familiar with the following basic map components:

- A legend or key defines the symbols on the map.
- A compass rose shows cardinal directions—north, south, east, west.
- A scale shows the ratio between distances on the map and actual distances on Earth.

Reading Strategy

Using Maps for Verification and Interpretation

To **verify and interpret** information is to check whether it is true and to explore its significance. To verify and interpret textual information using a map, follow the steps below:

1. Identify claims in the text for which geographical information is relevant.
2. Formulate geographical questions based on the text.
3. Obtain a map of the region referenced in the text. Consider whether you need a map that focuses on a specific kind of information.
4. Use the map to answer your questions. Note any additional questions, and consult other sources for answers.

BUILD UNDERSTANDING

Knowing this term will help you read this map.

literary map *n.* map that focuses on the significance of geographical locations as they relate to literary works and authors. These maps often show where important authors were born, lived, and/or wrote.

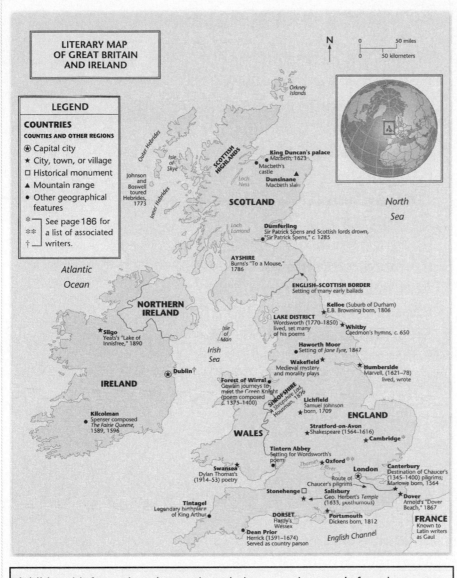

LITERARY MAP OF GREAT BRITAIN AND IRELAND

LEGEND

COUNTRIES
COUNTIES AND OTHER REGIONS
- ✸ Capital city
- ★ City, town, or village
- ☐ Historical monument
- ▲ Mountain range
- ● Other geographical features
- * See page 186 for
- ** a list of associated
- † writers.

N
0   50 miles
0   50 kilometers

Orkney Islands

Outer Hebrides

SCOTTISH HIGHLANDS

King Duncan's palace
Macbeth, 1623

Isle of Skye

Macbeth's castle

Johnson and Boswell toured Hebrides, 1773

Loch Ness

Dunsinane
Macbeth slain ▲

Inner Hebrides

SCOTLAND

North Sea

Atlantic Ocean

Loch Lomond

Dumferling
Sir Patrick Spens and Scottish lords drown,
"Sir Patrick Spens," c. 1285

AYSHIRE
Burns's "To a Mouse," 1786

ENGLISH–SCOTTISH BORDER
Setting of many early ballads

Kelloe (Suburb of Durham)
★ E.B. Browning born, 1806

LAKE DISTRICT
Wordsworth (1770–1850) lived, set many of his poems

★ **Whitby**
Caedmon's hymns, c. 650

NORTHERN IRELAND

★ **Sligo**
Yeats's "Lake of Innisfree," 1890

Isle of Man

Irish Sea

Haworth Moor
● Setting of *Jane Eyre,* 1847

Wakefield ★
Medieval mystery and morality plays

★ **Humberside**
Marvell, (1621–78) lived, wrote

✸ **Dublin** †

IRELAND

Forest of Wirral
Gawain journeys to meet the Green Knight (poem composed c. 1375–1400)

SHROPSHIRE
Shropshire Lad,
Housman's 1876

Lichfield
Samuel Johnson ★ born, 1709

ENGLAND

★ **Kilcolman**
Spenser composed *The Fairie Queene,* 1589, 1596

WALES

Stratford-on-Avon
★ Shakespeare (1564–1616)

★ **Cambridge** ✸

Tintern Abbey
Setting for Wordsworth's poem

Thames

★ **Oxford** ★

★ **Swansea**
Dylan Thomas's (1914–53) poetry

★ **London**
✸ Route of Chaucer's pilgrims

Canterbury
Destination of Chaucer's (1345–1400) pilgrims; Marlowe born, 1564

Stonehenge ☐

Salisbury
★ Geo. Herbert's *Temple* (1633, posthumous)

★ **Dover**
Arnold's "Dover Beach," 1867

★ **Tintagel**
Legendary birthplace of King Arthur #

DORSET
Hardy's Wessex

Portsmouth
Dickens born, 1812

FRANCE
Known to Latin writers as Gaul

● **Dean Prior**
Herrick (1591–1674) Served as country parson

English Channel

Additional information about selected places on the map is found on the next page.

◆ **Reading Maps**

A legend explains the symbols used on a **map**. What does a star inside a circle symbolize?

_____

_____

◆ **Culture Note**

The ballad, a poem or song that tells a story, is an important cultural and historic tradition of Great Britain. On the map, circle the English-Scottish border, the setting of many early ballads.

Mark the Text

◆ **Reading Strategy**

Using the map, **verify** the city, town, or village associated with William Shakespeare.

_____

_____

WRITERS ASSOCIATED WITH SELECTED PLACES IN GREAT BRITAIN AND IRELAND

*Cambridge
Authors who studied here include

1

Francis **Bacon** 1561–1626
Rupert **Brooke** 1887–1915
George Gordon, Lord **Byron** 1788–1824

5

Samuel Taylor **Coleridge** 1772–1834
John **Dryden** 1631–1700
E.M. **Forster** 1879–1970
Thomas **Gray** 1716–1771
George **Herbert** 1593–1633

10

Robert **Herrick** 1591–1674
Christopher **Marlowe** 1564–1593
Andrew **Marvell** 1621–1678
Samuel **Pepys** 1633–1703
Siegfried **Sassoon** 1886–1967

15

Edmund **Spenser** 1552?–1599
Alfred, Lord **Tennyson** 1809–1892
William **Wordsworth** 1770–1850
Sir Thomas **Wyatt** 1503–1542

**Oxford

20

Authors who studied here include

Joseph **Addison** 1672–1719
Matthew **Arnold** 1822–1888
John **Donne** 1572–1631
T. S. **Eliot** 1888–1965

25

Gerard Manley **Hopkins** 1844–1889
A.E. **Housman** 1859–1936
Samuel **Johnson** 1709–1784
Richard **Lovelace** 1618–1657

Louis **MacNeice** 1907–1963
Sir Walter **Raleigh** 1552–1618
Percy Bysshe **Shelley** 1792–1822
Sir Philip **Sidney** 1554–1586
Richard **Steele** 1672–1729

35 **†Dublin**
Authors associated with the city include

James **Joyce** 1882–1941
George Bernard **Shaw** 1856–1950
Sir Richard **Steele** 1672–1729
40 Jonathan **Swift** 1667–1745
Oscar **Wilde** 1854–1900
William Butler **Yeats** 1865–1939

◆ **Read Fluently**

Read aloud the list of authors associated with the city of Dublin. If any of these authors are familiar to you, circle their names.

Reading Informational Materials

In what ways would a tourist **map** of Great Britain and Ireland be similar to and different from this literary map? Write two similarities and two differences.

Similarities:

1. _____

_____

2. _____

_____

Differences:

1. _____

_____

2. _____

_____

Check Your Comprehension

1. What is the purpose of the Literary Map of Great Britain and Ireland?

_____

2. Determine the direction from Oxford to King Duncan's palace.

_____

3. In what part of England did the poet John Donne study?

_____

Applying the Reading Strategy

Using Maps for Verification and Interpretation

4. Give two examples of information you might verify or interpret with a literary map.

_____

_____

Writing Informational Materials

Pick three authors whom you would include on a literary map of the United States or of a section of the United States. Then, using reference sources, find out where they were born, where they wrote, or what geographic areas are prominently featured in their work.

Author: _____

Geographic locations: _____

Author: _____

Geographic locations: _____

Author: _____

Geographic locations: _____

About Position Statements

A **position statement** is an essay that presents the views of an individual or group on a particular issue. It features the following elements:

- An introductory statement that identifies the issue and the writer's position
- Arguments in support of the position
- The use of support such as expert opinions and statistics

In this position statement, *The Defense of Poesy*, Sir Philip Sidney (1554–1586) defends art against those who criticize it.

Reading Strategy

Analyzing Expert Opinions and Allusions

As you read position statements, identify the evidence the author uses in support of an opinion; and determine how it supports the author's position:

- **Expert opinions** are judgments made by people who have studied an issue extensively. In *The Defense*, for example, Sidney refers to the opinions of a respected authority on art, the Greek philosopher Aristotle.
- **Allusions** are brief references to literary works and historical figures. Because Sidney's subject is literature, he uses allusions as examples to support his points. He also gains authority for his points by alluding to respected authors, such as the ancient poet Homer.

BUILD UNDERSTANDING

Knowing these words will help you read this position statement.

poesy (POH uh see) *n.* old-fashioned term for poetry. Here it is used to define all types of literature.

precept (PREE sept) *n.* rule of conduct

---

from The Defense of Poesy
Sir Philip Sidney

Nature never set forth the earth in so rich tapestry as divers poets have done, neither with so pleasant rivers, fruitful trees, sweet-smelling flowers, nor whatsoever else may make the too much loved earth more lovely. Her world is brazen,[1] the poets only deliver a golden. But let those things alone, and go to man (for whom as the other things are, so it seems in him her uttermost cunning is employed), and know whether she have brought forth so true a lover as Theagenes, so constant a friend as Pylades, so valiant a man as Orlando, so right a prince as Xenophon's Cyrus, and so excellent a man every way as Virgil's Aeneas.[2] Neither let this be jestingly conceived because the works of the one be essential, the other in imitation or fiction, for every understanding knows the skill of each artificer stands in that Idea or foreconceit of the work, and not in the work itself. And that the poet has that Idea is manifest, by delivering them forth in such excellency as he had imagined them. Which delivering forth also is not wholly imaginative, as we are wont to say by them that build castles in the air, but so far substantially it works, not only to make a Cyrus, which had been but a particular excellence, as Nature might have done, but to bestow a Cyrus upon the world to make many Cyruses, if they will learn aright why and how that maker made him.

. . .

The philosopher . . . and the historian are they which would win the goal, the one by precept, the other by example. But both, not having both, do both

1

5

10

15

20

25

---

1. **brazen** (BRAY zuhn) *adj.* made of brass, a metal alloy of inferior value to gold.
2. **Theagenes . . . Aeneas** Heroes of ancient Greek, ancient Roman, and medieval literature and histories.

halt. For the philosopher, setting down with thorny arguments the bare rule, is so hard of utterance, and so misty to be conceived, that one that has no other guide but him shall wade in him till he be old before he shall find sufficient cause to be honest: for his

35 knowledge stands so upon the abstract and general, that happy is that man who may understand him, and more happy that can apply what he does understand. On the other side, the historian, wanting the precept, is so tied, not to what should be but to what is, to the

40 particular truth of things and not to the general reason of things, that his example draws no necessary consequence, and therefore a less fruitful doctrine.

Now does the peerless poet perform both: for whatsoever the philosopher says should be done, he

45 gives a perfect picture of it by some one by whom he presupposes it was done; so as he couples the general notion with the particular example. A perfect picture, I say, for he yields to the powers of the mind an image of that whereof the philosopher bestows

50 but a wordish description, which does neither strike, pierce, nor possess the sight of the soul so much as that other does.

© Pearson Education, Inc.

◆ **Vocabulary and Pronunciation**

The underlined word *presupposes* contains the prefix *pre-*, which means "before." *Presupposes* means "to suppose, or assume, beforehand." Write the meanings of the words below, which contain the prefix *pre-*.

preview _____

_____

prepare _____

_____

predict _____

_____

Reading Informational Materials

Often the goal of a **position paper** is to persuade readers to share a particular viewpoint. Do you think the writer of *The Defense of Poesy* is successful in his attempt to persuade readers?

_____

Why or why not?

_____

_____

_____

_____

Check Your Comprehension

1. Write the correct word on each line to complete the statement below.

poetry   **history**   **philosophy**

The writer says that _____ offers only words and _____

offers only facts. Therefore, _____ is the most inspiring.

Applying the Reading Strategy

Analyzing Expert Opinions and Allusions

2. Who are three classic heroes the writer alludes to in this essay?

_____

3. Does the writer assume his audience is familiar with

Cyrus? _____ Explain. _____

_____

Writing Informational Materials

Complete the outline below by identifying an issue that is important to you, such as the right to free speech or the right to another freedom. Write your position, or opinion about this issue. Then, list three details that support your position. Finally, write a concluding statement that sums up your ideas.

Issue: _____

Position: _____

Supporting Detail 1: _____

Supporting Detail 2: _____

Supporting Detail 3: _____

Concluding Statement: _____

On a separate sheet of paper, use this outline to write a brief position statement.

About Scientific Reports

Scientific reports describe the results of experiments or offer scientific explanations for natural events. An informative scientific report presents the following information:

1. A description of the pattern of events under investigation
2. A hypothesis—or educated guess—that attempts to explain why these events occur
3. A detailed description of the steps taken to test the hypothesis
4. A statement of results and general conclusions drawn from the research

Reading Strategy

Evaluating Scientific Reasoning

By **evaluating scientific reasoning,** you can get a sense of the importance of a certain scientific experiment. A well-designed experiment focuses on a basic scientific question, then methodically eliminates all possible explanations except one. As you read Sir Isaac Newton's scientific report, evaluate his scientific reasoning by keeping the following questions in mind:

1. Is Newton's scientific question well defined?
2. Does Newton examine multiple possibilities and explanations?
3. Does Newton draw sound conclusions based on experimental results?

BUILD UNDERSTANDING

Knowing these terms will help you understand this scientific report.

triangular glass prism a glass object, shaped like a pyramid, that bends light and separates it into the colors of a rainbow

refracted (ri FRAKT id) *v.* bent when passing from one medium to another (as from air to glass)

colored spectrum a band of colors made up of six different wavelengths of light

---

Letter on Light and Color
Sir Isaac Newton

Letter sent to the Royal Society

February 6, 1672

1

Sir,

To perform my late promise to you, I shall without further ceremony acquaint you that in the beginning of the year 1666 (at which time I applied myself to the grinding of optic glasses of other figures than spherical) I procured me a triangular glass prism to try therewith the celebrated phenomena of colors. And in order thereto having darkened my chamber and made a small hole in my window-shuts to let in a convenient quantity of the sun's light, I placed my prism at his entrance that it might be thereby refracted to the opposite wall. It was at first a very pleasing divertissement to view the vivid and intense colors produced thereby; but after a while, applying myself to consider more circumspectly, I became surprised to see them in an *oblong*[1] form, which according to the received laws of refraction I expected should have been *circular*.

They were terminated at the sides with straight lines, but at the ends the decay of light was so gradual that it was difficult to determine justly what was their figure; yet they seemed *semicircular*.

Comparing the length of this colored spectrum with its breadth, I found it about five times greater, a disproportion so extravagant that it excited me to a more than ordinary curiosity of examining from whence it might proceed. I could scarce think that the various thickness of the glass or the termination with shadow or darkness could have any influence on light to produce such an effect; yet I thought it not amiss first to examine those circumstances, and so

---

1. **oblong** (AHB lawng) *adj.* rectangular.

tried what would happen by transmitting light through parts of the glass of divers thicknesses, or by setting the prism without so that the light might pass
35 through it and be refracted before it was terminated by the hole. But I found none of those circumstances material. The fashion of the colors was in all these cases the same.

Then I suspected whether by any unevenness in
40 the glass or other contingent irregularity these colors might be thus dilated. And to try this, I took another prism like the former and so placed it that the light, passing through them both, might be refracted contrary ways, and so by the latter returned into that
45 course from which the former had diverted it. For by this means I thought the regular effects of the first prism would be destroyed by the second prism but the irregular ones more augmented by the multiplicity of refractions. The event was that the light which by the first prism was diffused into an oblong form was by the second reduced into an orbicular[2] one with as much regularity as when it did not at all pass through them. So that, whatever was the cause of that length, 'twas not any contingent irregularity.

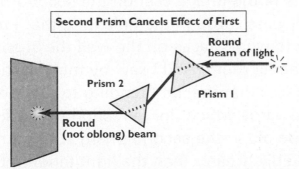

Second Prism Cancels Effect of First

Round beam of light

Prism 2

Prism I

Round (not oblong) beam

. . .

55 The gradual removal of these suspicions at length led me to the *experimentum crucis*,[3] which was this: I took two boards, and placed one of them close behind the prism at the window, so that the light

2. **orbicular** (or BIK yoo ler) *adj.* circular.
3. **experimentum crucis** the most crucial, or important, experiment.

◆ **Reading Strategy**

Mark the Text

Evaluate Newton's scientific reasoning in the bracketed paragraph by answering the following questions:

1. What phase of the investigation is this?

a) Asking a basic scientific question

b) Testing possibilities

c) Publishing final results

_____

2. Look closely at the diagram. Two identical prisms held at opposite angles change the ray of light back to its original state. If the first prism had an imperfection, would the beam of light on the wall still be round?

_____

Underline the words in the text that support your answer.

Use the diagram to **evaluate the scientific reasoning** behind Newton's "critical experiment." What is the difference between the way A and B are set up?

_____

_____

_____

Why might Newton set up two slightly different experiments?

_____

_____

_____

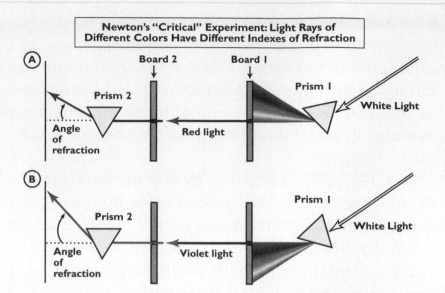

Newton's "Critical" Experiment: Light Rays of Different Colors Have Different Indexes of Refraction

◆ **Reading Check**

Read the bracketed passage. Underline the sentence that shows what Newton saw as a result of this experiment.

might pass through a small hole made in it for the purpose and fall on the other board, which I placed   60
at about 12 feet distance, having first made a small hole in it also, for some of that incident light to pass through. Then I placed another prism behind this second board so that the light, through both the boards, might pass through that also, and be again refracted before it arrived at the wall. This done, I took the first prism in my hand, and turned it to and fro slowly about its axis, so much as to make the several parts of the image cast on the second board successively pass through the hole in it, that I might   70
observe to what places on the wall the second prism would refract them. And I saw by the variation of those places that the light tending to that end of the image towards which the refraction of the first prism was made did in the second prism suffer a refraction   75
considerably greater than the light tending to the other end. And so the true cause of the length of that image was detected to be no other than that light consists of *rays differently refrangible*,[4] which, without any respect to a difference in their incidence,[5]   80

---

4. **refrangible** (ri FRAN juh buhl) *adj.* able to be refracted, or bent.
5. **incidence** (IN suh duhns) *n.* the way a ray of light hits an object.

were, according to their degrees of refrangibility, transmitted towards divers parts of the wall.

. . .

Newton sums up his conclusions.

1. As the rays of light differ in degrees of refrangibility, so they also differ in their disposition to exhibit this or that particular color. Colors are not qualifications of light, derived from refractions or reflections of natural bodies (as 'tis generally believed), but original and connate properties which in divers rays are divers.[6] Some rays are disposed to exhibit a red color and no other; some a yellow and no other, some a green and no other, and so of the rest. Nor are there only rays proper and particular to the more eminent colors, but even to all their intermediate gradations.

2. To the same degree of refrangibility ever belongs the same color, and to the same color ever belongs the same degree of refrangibility. The least refrangible rays are all disposed to exhibit a red color, and contrarily those rays which are disposed to exhibit a red color are all the least refrangible. So the most refrangible rays are all disposed to exhibit a deep violet color, and contrarily those which are apt to exhibit such a violet color are all the most refrangible. And so to all the intermediate colors in a continued series belong intermediate degrees of refrangibility. And this analogy 'twixt colors and refrangibility is very precise and strict; the rays always exactly agreeing in both or proportionally disagreeing in both.

◆ **Read Fluently**

Read conclusion #1. Which statement is supported by the conclusion?

a. A prism bends purple and red light at exactly the same angle.

b. A prism bends purple and red light at different angles.

◆ **Read Fluently**

Read conclusion #2 aloud. Which statement is supported by the conclusion?

a. The angle of refraction of green light is always the same.

b. The angle at which green light is refracted depends on the brightness of the light.

Reading Informational Materials

Research reports can point the way to a new understanding of the natural world. With this experiment, what did Newton prove was measurable and constant?

a. the amount of light hitting the prism

b. the angle that light is bent for each color

---

6. **Colors are not . . . are divers** Objects do not add color to light. Instead, color is an essential quality of light itself. (In modern terms: Different wavelengths of light are each a different color.)

Check Your Comprehension

1. List two hypotheses that Newton tests, then rejects.

_____

_____

2. (a) Why does Newton decide to shine light through two prisms?

_____

(b) What results does he get?

_____

(c) What conclusions does he draw?

_____

Applying the Reading Strategy

Evaluating Scientific Reasoning

3. One standard for judging a scientific experiment is the ability for other scientists to carry out the same experiment, obtain the same results, and draw similar conclusions. What parts of Newton's report could scientists use to confirm his results?

_____

_____

4. A scientific report should be clear and understandable. However, this report was written in the seventeenth century. Which parts of Newton's report meet this standard for today's readers?

_____

Which do not? _____

_____

Writing Informational Materials

Think of a simple scientific experiment you have done in school. On a separate sheet of paper, write a brief scientific report describing the experiment. Be sure to include all the parts of a scientific report—framing a question, forming hypotheses, testing hypotheses, reporting results, and drawing conclusions.

About Book Reviews

A response to literature is a piece of writing that discusses a reader's reaction to a work. One type of response to literature is a **book review**. Book reviews include the following elements:

- The reviewer's reactions to and insights about a work
- General observations about works of this type
- Insight into the relationship of the work to the writer's life or to other works
- A recommendation to readers about the work

Reading Strategy

Analyzing a Writer's Basic Assumptions

Assumptions are ideas, such as facts or guiding principles, that are taken for granted. A good book reviewer uses a rich set of assumptions about what is important in literary writing. Applying these assumptions to a book, the critic can measure its value. To help you identify and **analyze a writer's assumptions**, ask yourself these questions as you read:

1. To what general ideas, such as originality or good taste, does the reviewer repeatedly refer?
2. What powerful terms does the reviewer use to evaluate the work? Look for words like *compelling* or *sentimental*.
3. Which of these ideas and terms does the reviewer use in a positive sense? Which are used in a negative sense?

BUILD UNDERSTANDING

Knowing these words will help you read the book review.

diction (DIK shuhn) *n.* a writer's choice of words or style of expression

mannerists (MAN uhr ists) *n.* artists using an exaggerated or artificial style

tact (TAKT) *n.* perception of the right thing to do or say without offending people

---

Poet William Wordsworth (1770–1850) grew up in the Lake District of England. His great love of nature inspired his style of poetry, which was very different from other poetry of his time.

◆ Reading Book Reviews

In the opening of the **book review**, Jeffrey refers to Wordsworth and other Romantic poets as "mannerists." He means that the poets have decided consciously to draw attention to their poetry by using nonpoetic language. Is "mannerists" a negative or a positive term? Explain.

_____

_____

_____

_____

◆ Reading Strategy

In the bracketed passage, the writer states his **basic assumptions** about Wordsworth's poetry by contrasting negative and positive terms. Circle two negative terms. Underline two positive terms.

Early Reviews of Wordsworth

Francis Jeffrey

Book reviews,
The Edinburgh Review, 1807 and 1814

With Mr. Wordsworth and his friends, it is plain that their peculiarities of diction are things of choice, and not of accident. They write as they do, upon principle and system; and it evidently costs them much pains to keep *down* to the standard which they have proposed to themselves. They are, to the full, as much mannerists, too, as the poetasters[1] who ring changes on the commonplaces of magazine versification; and all the difference between them is, that they borrow their phrases from a different and scantier *gradus ad Parnassum*.[2] If they were, indeed, to discard all imitation and set phraseology, and to bring in no words merely for show or for meter—as much, perhaps, might be gained in freedom and originality, as would infallibly be lost in allusion and authority; but, in point of fact, the new poets are just as great borrowers as the old; only that, instead of borrowing from the more popular passages of their illustrious predecessors, they have preferred furnishing themselves from vulgar ballads and plebeian nurseries.

. . .

1

5

10

15

20

---

1. **poetasters** (POH uht AS tuhrz) *n.* inferior poets.
2. *gradus ad Parnassum* (GRAY duhs ad pahr NAS oom) *n.* dictionary for writing poetry (Latin for "step to Parnassus," mountain of Apollo and the Muses, deities of the arts).

Long habits of seclusion, and an excessive ambition of originality, can alone account for the disproportion which seems to exist between this author's
taste and his genius; or for the devotion with which
he has sacrificed so many precious gifts at the shrine
of those paltry idols which he has set up for himself
among his lakes and his mountains. Solitary mus-
ings, amidst such scenes, might no doubt be expected to nurse up the mind to the majesty of poetical
conception (though it is remarkable, that all the
greater poets lived, or had lived, in the full current of
society), but the collision of equal minds—the admo-
nition of prevailing impressions—seems necessary to
reduce its redundancies, and repress that tendency to
extravagance or puerility, . . . An habitual and general
knowledge of the few settled and permanent max-
ims, which form the canon[3] of general taste in all
large and polished societies—a certain tact, which
informs us at once that many things, which we still
love and are moved by in secret, must necessarily be
despised as childish, or derided as absurd, in all such
societies—though it will not stand in the place of
genius, seems necessary to the success of its exer-
tions; and though it will never enable anyone to produce the higher beauties of art, can alone secure the
talent which does produce them, from errors that
must render it useless. Those who have most of the
talent, however, commonly acquire this knowledge

◆ **Reading Check**

According to Jeffrey, in
what kind of surroundings
did Wordsworth live?

_____

_____

_____

◆ **Reading Check**

Jeffrey believes
that the key to
successful
poetry is
genius guided
by tact.

Underline words or
phrases in the bracketed
section that support this
idea.

---

3. **canon** (KAN uhn) *n.* group of established, basic rules.

Read the bracketed section to **analyze the writer's assumptions** about Wordsworth's life and surroundings. Does Jeffrey think these factors had a negative or positive effect on the poet's work? Explain.

_____

_____

_____

_____

Reading Informational Materials

Would you say that this **book review** is generally positive or generally negative?

_____

Explain.

_____

_____

_____

with the greatest facility; and if Mr. Wordsworth, instead of confining himself almost entirely to the society of the dalesmen[4] and cottagers and little children, who form the subjects of his book, had condescended to mingle a little more with the people that were to read and judge of it, we cannot help thinking that its texture might have been considerably improved: at least it appears to us to be absolutely impossible, that anyone who had lived or mixed familiarly with men of literature and ordinary judgment in poetry, (of course we exclude the coadjutors[5] and disciples of his own school) could ever have fallen into such gross faults, or so long mistaken them for beauties. His first essays we looked upon in a good degree as poetical paradoxes— maintained experimentally, in order to display talent, and court notoriety;—and so maintained, with no more serious belief in their truth, than is usually generated by an ingenious and animated defense of other paradoxes. But when we find that he has been for twenty years exclusively employed upon articles of this very fabric, and that he has still enough of raw material on hand to keep him so employed for twenty years to come, we cannot refuse him the justice of believing that he is a sincere convert to his own system. . . .

55

60

65

70

---

4. **dalesmen** simple farmers.
5. **coadjutors** (koh AJ uh terz) _n._ assistants.

Check Your Comprehension

1. Judging from this review, what details of Wordsworth's poetry made his work revolutionary at the time?

_____

2. According to Jeffrey, what aspects of Wordsworth's life shaped the style and content of his poetry?

_____

_____

Applying the Reading Strategy

Analyzing a Writer's Basic Assumptions

3. Does Jeffrey agree that Wordsworth's poetry has originality? Explain. _____

_____

4. What words does Jeffrey use to define good poetry?

_____

Writing Informational Materials

Define your own assumptions for judging poetry by answering the questions that follow.

What terms and ideas represent the poems you like best?

_____

_____

What terms and ideas represent the pocms you like least?

_____

_____

Using this information, write a short review of your favorite poem on another piece of paper.

READING INFORMATIONAL MATERIALS

WEB SITES

About Web Sites

A **Web site** is a specific location on the global network of computers known as the Internet. Companies or individuals post Web pages on the Internet so that computer users can access important information. A typical Web site consists of a main page, or *home page*, which is connected to a more extensive set of pages. The home page usually contains a site map and provides general information about the company or individual. Secondary pages contain detailed information. All Web pages have the ability to combine pictures, text, sound, and video.

Reading Strategy

Evaluating Credibility of Sources

An enormous amount of information is available on the Internet. Not all of this information, however, is accurate or of high quality. To use Web sites effectively, always **evaluate the credibility**, or believability, of the information first. You can evaluate credibility by asking the following questions:

* What are the qualifications of the authors who present the information?
* Do the authors' backgrounds influence the facts they choose to present?
* Can the information be confirmed by checking other sources?

As you view the Victorian Web site, think about how you would evaluate the credibility of the information it presents.

BUILD UNDERSTANDING

Knowing these terms will help you understand this Web site.

Victorian (vik TOR ee uhn) *adj.* the name given to an era of English history that spanned the reign of Queen Victoria (1837–1901)

WWW World Wide Web, the part of the Internet in which all Web sites are located

---

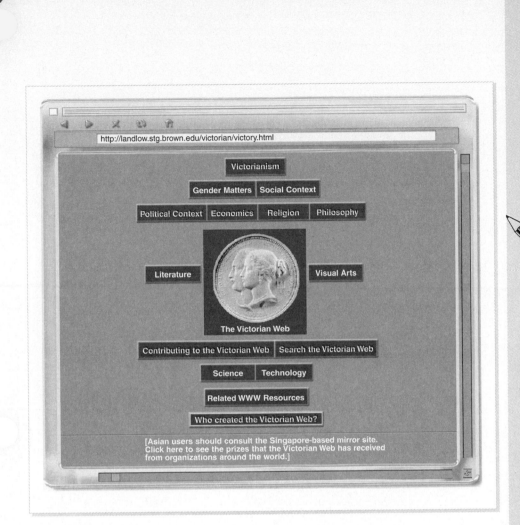

The Victorian Web

URL: http://landlow.stg.brown.edu/victorian/victory.html

- Victorianism
- Gender Matters
- Social Context
- Political Context
- Economics
- Religion
- Philosophy
- Literature
- Visual Arts
- Contributing to the Victorian Web
- Search the Victorian Web
- Science
- Technology
- Related WWW Resources
- Who created the Victorian Web?

[Asian users should consult the Singapore-based mirror site. Click here to see the prizes that the Victorian Web has received from organizations around the world.]

◆ **Stop to Reflect**

A group of links on a home page is often referred to as a *site map*. Why is the term *map* appropriate?

_____

_____

◆ **Culture Note**

Two prominent figures in Victorian England were the novelist Charles Dickens and the surgeon Joseph Lister. With his popular novels, Dickens brought attention to the problems facing the poor. Lister cut the rate of deaths in half at Victorian hospitals by demanding that surgical instruments be properly cleaned before surgery. Circle the two links that would display information on these two famous men.

◆ **Reading Strategy**

How could you use the last two links on this home page to **evaluate the credibility** of the information on this Web site?

_____

_____

_____

_____

Circle George P. Landow's title. How does knowing his title help you **evaluate the credibility** of the site?

_____

_____

_____

◆ **Read Fluently**

Web sites, like other media sources, sometimes provide lists of funders. Read the underlined sentence aloud. Why is it important to know who is paying for a source of factual information?

_____

_____

_____

Reading Informational Materials

Scholarly **Web sites** often include references to published writings. Read the bracketed section. Why does the reference to Anthony Wohl's published writings carry more weight than a reference to his unpublished writings would carry?

_____

_____

_____

_____

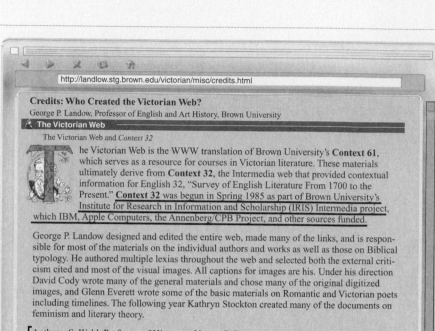

Credits: Who Created the Victorian Web?
George P. Landow, Professor of English and Art History, Brown University

The Victorian Web

The Victorian Web and *Context 32*

The Victorian Web is the WWW translation of Brown University's **Context 61**, which serves as a resource for courses in Victorian literature. These materials ultimately derive from **Context 32**, the Intermedia web that provided contextual information for English 32, "Survey of English Literature From 1700 to the Present." **Context 32** was begun in Spring 1985 as part of Brown University's Institute for Research in Information and Scholarship (IRIS) Intermedia project, which IBM, Apple Computers, the Annenberg/CPB Project, and other sources funded.

George P. Landow designed and edited the entire web, made many of the links, and is responsible for most of the materials on the individual authors and works as well as those on Biblical typology. He authored multiple lexias throughout the web and selected both the external criticism cited and most of the visual images. All captions for images are his. Under his direction David Cody wrote many of the general materials and chose many of the original digitized images, and Glenn Everett wrote some of the basic materials on Romantic and Victorian poets including timelines. The following year Kathryn Stockton created many of the documents on feminism and literary theory.

Anthony S. Wohl, Professor of History at Vassar College, generously contributed much of the material on Victorian public health, race and class issues, and anti-Catholic prejudice in Victorian England. This work draws upon both his published and unpublished writings.

Check Your Comprehension

1. **(a)** Who created this Web site?

   _____

   (b) In what subject area is he an expert?

   _____

2. Who wrote materials on Romantic and Victorian poets?

   _____

Applying the Reading Strategy

Evaluating Credibility of Sources

3. Explain whether or not you would think materials written by Professor Landow were more credible than materials written by his students.

   _____

   _____

4. Look at the titles of Landow and Wohl. Then, name two links on the home page that you would be inclined to trust. Name two links you would consider more cautiously. Explain your reasoning.

   _____

   _____

   _____

   _____

Using Informational Materials

   Choose a topic of interest to you. Imagine you were asked to design a Web site on that topic. On a separate piece of paper, write down a list of links you would include on the home page, as well as a description of the art you would use.

About Mission Statements

Suppose that you want to do some volunteer work for a charitable organization. To learn the group's objectives, you might read its mission statement. A **mission statement** is a document provided by a group to identify itself and describe its objectives and daily activities. A mission statement helps introduce the organization to the general public. It can also help a nonprofit organization obtain government grants.

Reading Strategy

Interpreting the Organization of a Mission Statement

The **organization of a mission statement** is important to its success. To engage casual readers, the statement must make basic information easy to find. It should also contain enough facts to satisfy those who desire specific information. The following organizational strategies are commonly used in mission statements:

- Short and concise boldface subheads to help readers find main points
- Short, focused paragraphs and groups of bulleted items to help readers follow ideas easily
- Points arranged in order of importance to focus readers' attention
- Details arranged in chronological order to allow readers to see what steps are taken to accomplish objectives

BUILD UNDERSTANDING

Knowing these terms will help you read this mission statement.

United Kingdom a region made up of Great Britain (England, Wales, and Scotland) and Northern Ireland

disseminate (di SEM i NAYT) *v.* to scatter or spread far and wide

The National Gallery
Role and Objectives

1 **Role**

The National Gallery houses the national Collection of Western European paintings from around 1250 to 1900.

5 The Gallery's aim is to care for, enhance and study its Collection, so as to offer the fullest access to the pictures for the education and enjoyment of the widest possible public now and in the future. It aims for the highest international standards in all its

10 activities.

The Collection belongs to the people of the United Kingdom. It is open, free of charge, to all.

The Gallery serves a very wide and diverse public, which includes:

15
- those who visit the Gallery of London—both those who visit frequently and those who visit only occasionally;
- those who see its pictures while they are on loan elsewhere, both inside and outside the UK, and

20 those who know the Collection through publications, multimedia and TV;
- those who live nearby as well as those who live further away in the United Kingdom and overseas;

◆ Read Fluently

Read the bracketed passage aloud. Then, in your own words, explain the National Gallery's role as it is stated in the **mission statement**.

_____
_____
_____
_____

◆ Reading Strategy

Do you think the use of boldface headings and bulleted items make the mission statement easy to read? Explain.

_____
_____
_____

What other kinds of materials use **organizational features** like these to convey information to readers?

_____
_____
_____

◆ **Vocabulary and Pronunciation**

In English, the prefix *un-* means "not." For example, the underlined word *uninformed* means "not informed." Based on this information, write the meanings of the following words:

1. unfriendly

_____

2. unqualified

_____

3. unintentional

_____

◆ **Reading Strategy**

What type of **organization**—order of importance or chronological order—is used in the bulleted list under "Care for the Collection"?

_____

_____

◆ **Reading Check**

Does the museum encourage students to conduct research in the gallery? Circle the phrases in the text that support your answer.

- every age group—from children to pensioners;
- the socially excluded and the privileged; the <u>uninformed</u> and the specialist; and those with special needs;
- the worldwide community of museums and galleries;
- and, most importantly, future generations.

Objectives

The Gallery aims to:

Care for the Collection

- keep the pictures in the nation's Collection safe for future generations by maintaining a secure and appropriate environment for them, monitoring their condition regularly, and undertaking suitable restoration or conservation;
- do everything possible to secure the pictures from fire, theft and other hazards;
- do everything possible to ensure that pictures loaned out are in sound enough condition to travel safely.

Enhance the Collection

- acquire great pictures across the whole range of European painting to enhance the Collection now and for future generations.

Study the Collection

- encourage all aspects of scholarship on the Collection, researching and documenting the pictures to the highest international standards, and ensuring that this work is disseminated.

Provide Access to the Collection for the Education and Enjoyment of the Widest Possible Public

- encourage the public to use the Collection as their own by maintaining free admission, during the most convenient possible hours, to as much as possible of the permanent Collection;

- display the pictures well;
- promote knowledge of the Collection and encourage the public to visit it;
- help the widest possible public both in the Gallery and beyond to understand and enjoy the paintings, taking advantage of the opportunities created by modern technology;
- offer the highest possible standards in services for our visitors.

Stand as a National and International Leader in All Its Activities

- work with other regional museums and galleries in the United Kingdom;
- enhance the national and international standing of the Gallery.

65

70

Reading Informational Materials

The bulleted list on page 208 describes strategies for organizing **mission statements**. Does the National Gallery use these strategies effectively in its mission statement?

_____

Explain.

_____

_____

_____

_____

Check Your Comprehension

1. Who owns the National Gallery's Collection?

_____

2. How is the National Gallery going to enhance its Collection in the future?

_____

_____

3. What is the general purpose of the National Gallery?

_____

Applying the Reading Strategy

Organizing a Mission Statement

4. Does grouping related details help provide a more clearly defined mission statement? Explain.

_____

_____

5. Does the organization of this mission statement help you understand the National Gallery's goals and objectives?

_____

Explain.

_____

_____

Writing Informational Materials

Many high schools have a number of clubs and societies. Choose an organization in your school with which you are familiar. Write a mission statement for it on another sheet of paper. Use at least two of the organizational strategies described on p. 208.

VOCABULARY BUILDER

As you read the selections in this book, you will come across many unfamiliar words. Mark these words and look them up in a dictionary. Then use these pages to record the words you want to remember. Write the word, the selection in which it appears, its part of speech, and its definition. Then, use the word in an original sentence that demonstrates its meaning.

Try to use these new words in your writing and speech. Using the words regularly will help you make them part of your everyday vocabulary.

Word: _____ Page: _____

Selection: _____

Part of speech: _____

Definition: _____

_____

Original Sentence: _____

_____

_____

Word: _____ Page: _____

Selection: _____

Part of speech: _____

Definition: _____

_____

Original Sentence: _____

_____

_____

Word: _____ Page: _____

Selection: _____

Part of speech: _____

Definition: _____

_____

Original Sentence: _____

_____

_____

Word: _____ Page: _____

Selection: _____

Part of speech: _____

Definition: _____

_____

Original Sentence: _____

_____

_____

Word: _____ Page: _____

Selection: _____

Part of speech: _____

Definition: _____

_____

Original Sentence: _____

_____

_____

Word: _____ Page: _____

Selection: _____

Part of speech: _____

Definition: _____

_____

Original Sentence: _____

_____

_____

Word: _____ Page: _____

Selection: _____

Part of speech: _____

Definition: _____

_____

Original Sentence: _____

_____

_____

Word: _____ Page: _____

Selection: _____

Part of speech: _____

Definition: _____

_____

Original Sentence: _____

_____

_____

Word:_____ Page: _____

Selection: _____

Part of speech: _____

Definition: _____

_____

Original Sentence: _____

_____

_____

Word:_____ Page: _____

Selection: _____

Part of speech: _____

Definition: _____

_____

Original Sentence: _____

_____

_____

Word:_____ Page: _____

Selection: _____

Part of speech: _____

Definition: _____

_____

Original Sentence: _____

_____

_____

Word: _____ Page: _____

Selection: _____

Part of speech: _____

Definition: _____

_____

Original Sentence: _____

_____

_____

Word: _____ Page: _____

Selection: _____

Part of speech: _____

Definition: _____

_____

Original Sentence: _____

_____

_____

Word: _____ Page: _____

Selection: _____

Part of speech: _____

Definition: _____

_____

Original Sentence: _____

_____

_____

Word: _____ Page: _____

Selection: _____

Part of speech: _____

Definition: _____

_____

Original Sentence: _____

_____

_____

Word: _____ Page: _____

Selection: _____

Part of speech: _____

Definition: _____

_____

Original Sentence: _____

_____

_____

Word: _____ Page: _____

Selection: _____

Part of speech: _____

Definition: _____

_____

Original Sentence: _____

_____

_____

If you run out of room, continue the Vocabulary Builder in your notebook.

Photo and Art Credits